ך אשר בשערך ‏ ‏ ‏ ‏ ‏ ‏ למען ייטב עמך ואתן

ני עבד הייתה ‏ ‏ ‏ ‏ ‏ באדץ מצרים ויצאך

משם בכל ‏ ‏ ‏ ‏ ‏ ‏ ‏ חזקה ובזרע נטויה

א אלהיך ‏ ‏ ‏ ‏ ‏ ‏ ‏ לשמר את יום השבת

את ‏ ‏ ‏ ‏ ‏ ‏ ‏ ‏ ‏ ‏ ‏ ‏ ימים עשה יהוה ואת השמים ואת הארץ

אשר בם וינח ביום השביעי על כן ברך ואת

לקחשו ‏ ‏ ‏ ‏ ‏ כבד את אביך ואת אמך כאשן

לאהיך ‏ ‏ ‏ ‏ ‏ ‏ ‏ יטב לך ולמען יאריכן ומין ולמען ייטב

אשר יהוה ‏ ‏ ‏ ‏ אלהיך נתן לך לא ‏ ‏ ‏ ‏ ‏ תרצח לא

ב לא תענה ברעך עד שוא לא תגנב ואתחמד

א תחמד בת רעיך שדה עבדך אמת

וכל אשר לרעך

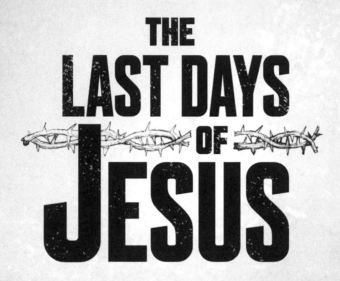

THE
LAST DAYS
OF
JESUS

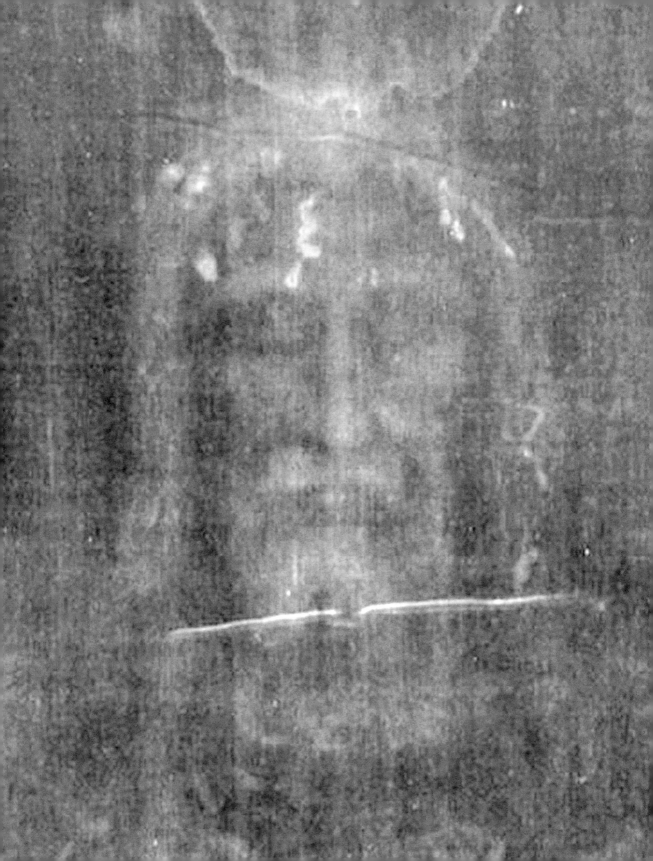

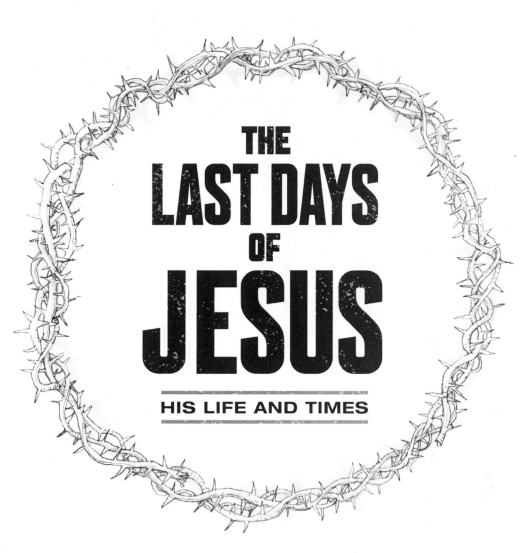

THE
LAST DAYS
OF
JESUS

HIS LIFE AND TIMES

Bill O'Reilly

with illustrations by William Low

Henry Holt and Company

✦ NEW YORK ✦

Henry Holt and Company, LLC
Publishers since 1866
175 Fifth Avenue
New York, New York 10010
mackids.com

Library of Congress Cataloging-in-Publication Data is available
ISBN 978-0-8050-9877-8

Henry Holt books may be purchased for business or promotional use. For information on bulk purchases,
please contact Macmillan Corporate and Premium Sales Department at (800) 221-7945 x5442
or by e-mail at specialmarkets@macmillan.com.

First Edition—2014
Based on the book *Killing Jesus* by Bill O'Reilly, published by Henry Holt and Company, LLC.
Designed by Meredith Pratt
Printed in the United States of America by R. R. Donnelley & Sons Company, Harrisonburg, Virginia

1 3 5 7 9 10 8 6 4 2

To Madeline and Spencer
who are following the path of Jesus

BOOK ONE

BOOK TWO

CONTENTS

BOOK THREE

THE LAST WEEK, DAY BY DAY

A NOTE TO READERS

In the Beginning . . .

JESUS OF NAZARETH IS CERTAINLY ONE OF THE MOST influential men who ever lived. Many people are sure that he is number one on that list. Nearly two thousand years after he was brutally murdered by Roman soldiers, more than 2.2 billion human beings attempt to follow his teachings and believe he is the Son of God. I am one of them, a Roman Catholic who was educated in religious schools all the way through college.

But I am also an historian who investigates the truth about important people. That is what I have done in this book. I believe that in order to understand what Jesus accomplished and why he paid with his life, we have to understand what was happening around him. It was a time when Rome dominated the western world and allowed no dissent. Human life was worth little. Life expectancy was less than forty years and far less if you happened to anger the Romans.

For evidence about Jesus's life, we look to the New Testament gospels, accounts written by four of his friends. Admittedly these narratives concentrate on the evidence that Jesus was God, but we can gather facts about his life and times in them as well. In addition, the Romans kept good records of the time and a few Jewish historians also wrote down the events of the day.

From these, I have gathered information and written a fact-based book about Jesus the man. I do not address Jesus as the Messiah, but as a man who inspired people in a remote part of the Roman Empire by preaching a philosophy of peace and love and who made very powerful enemies at the same time. This is a violent story about the punishment this man received because he upset the ruling people in government and at his own temple.

I do not suggest that I know everything about Jesus. There are major gaps in his life, and at times I can only suppose what happened to him based upon best available evidence. The sources I used in researching the life of Jesus, and other books, websites, and DVDs that I think you might be interested in, are listed on the last pages of this book.

This is a story of the struggle between good and evil. Thank you for reading it.

New York
April 2014

KEY PLAYERS

THE FAMILY OF JESUS

JOSEPH: Husband of Mary.

MARY: Mother of Jesus.

JESUS

JESUS'S ORIGINAL DISCIPLES

MATTHEW: A tax collector.

SIMON (whom Jesus renamed Peter): A fisherman and one of Jesus's inner circle; very active in preaching to the Jews after Jesus's death.

ANDREW: Brother of Simon, a disciple of John the Baptist and then of Jesus; also a fisherman.

JUDAS ISCARIOT: The only disciple from Judea; betrayed Jesus for thirty pieces of silver.

PHILIP: A fisherman; preached in Samaria after Jesus's death.

BARTHOLOMEW (or Nathanael): Watched and listened to Jesus before finally becoming a disciple.

THOMAS: Sometimes called Doubting Thomas because he questioned Jesus's divinity.

JUDE (or Thaddeus): Brother of James the Younger.

JOHN THE BELOVED: Brother of James the Elder; thought to be the closest to Jesus; lived to an old age.

SIMON THE ZEALOT: From Cana; thought to be a Zealot, a member of an extreme nationalistic group that hated Roman law.

JAMES THE ELDER: Brother of John; one of Jesus's inner circle.

JAMES THE YOUNGER: Brother of Jude.

WRITERS OF THE BOOKS OF THE TANAKH, OR HEBREW BIBLE, WHO PROPHESIED THE COMING OF A SAVIOR

MOSES: Led the Israelites out of slavery in Egypt in about 1440 BC.

DAVID: King and poet who lived about 1000 BC.

HOSEA: King who lived about 750 to 715 BC.

MICAH: Lived about 750 to 686 BC.

ISAIAH: Lived about 740 to 681 BC.

ZECHARIAH: Lived about 520 to 480 BC.

PATRIARCHS OF THE JEWISH PEOPLE

ABRAHAM: According to Jewish tradition, the first to believe in one God.

DANIEL: A Jewish captive in Babylon who interpreted dreams and made prophecies.

DAVID: Second king of the Israelites, poet, and ancestor of Jesus.

ELIJAH: Prophet who foretold the coming of a Messiah.

ISAAC: The son Abraham was willing to sacrifice to prove his faith.

JACOB: One of Isaac's sons; believed to be the father of the Jewish people whose twelve sons founded the twelve tribes of Israel.

JEREMIAH: A prophet who warned of, and witnessed, the destruction of Jerusalem and the First Temple.

MOSES: The prophet who received the Ten Commandments from God and led the Jews out of Egypt.

SAMSON: A man of amazing strength who saved the Jews from the Philistines.

SOLOMON: Son of David; third king of the Israelites and builder of the First Temple.

ROMAN RULERS AND ADMINISTRATORS DURING JESUS'S LIFETIME

AUGUSTUS CAESAR: Emperor from 27 BC to AD 14.

TIBERIUS: Succeeded Augustus as emperor and ruled from AD 14 to 37.

PONTIUS PILATE: Roman prefect, or governor, of Judea from AD 26 to 36.

HEROD THE GREAT: Reigned as king of the province of Judea from 37 to 4 BC; rebuilt and renovated the Second Temple in Jerusalem.

HEROD ANTIPAS: One of Herod the Great's sons; a tetrarch, or administrator, of Galilee from 4 BC to AD 39.

TEMPLE PRIESTS AND RELIGIOUS GROUPS

ANNAS: Patriarch high priest; father-in-law of Caiaphas.

CAIAPHAS: High priest of the temple; one in a family of priests.

JOSEPH OF ARIMATHEA: Wealthy, influential Sadducee who became a secret disciple of Jesus and gave his tomb for Jesus's body.

NICODEMUS: Influential Pharisee who questioned Jesus and became a secret disciple.

PHARISEES: Less wealthy, more liberal priests.

SADDUCEES: High-born priests who believed in the letter of the Mosaic Law.

OTHERS

ANNA: Pilgrim at the temple who bore witness to the divinity of Jesus.

BARABBAS: Convicted thief who was freed as the people's choice over Jesus.

JOHN THE BAPTIST: Preacher who foretold the coming of the Messiah; baptized Jesus.

JUDAS OF GAMALA: Jewish revolutionary crucified in the early first century.

LAZARUS: Resident of Bethany who hosted Jesus and the disciples during their last Passover together.

MARY AND MARTHA: Sisters of Lazarus.

MARY OF MAGDALA: A devotee of Jesus; witnessed his death and anointed his body.

SIMEON: Pilgrim in the temple who declared Jesus to be the Son of God.

A CHANGING WORLD

63–6 BC ✦ JUDEA AND GALILEE

THE WORLD JESUS WAS BORN INTO WAS CHANGING. After hundreds of years of living a fairly consistent life under different invading armies, the Jews had been conquered by the Romans, who had altered the day-to-day life in Judea and Galilee. Long before the Romans, the Babylonians had invaded in 598 BC, followed by the Persians, the Egyptians, and the Syrians. In 63 BC, the Romans slowly advanced from their strongholds around the Mediterranean Sea, engulfing lands and peoples as they went.

And the Romans didn't take control peacefully. They invaded towns and cities, stealing land by simply occupying it. Soldiers in the Roman emperor's armies slaughtered anyone who put up a fight or got in their way, even members of groups traditionally considered off limits to civilized invaders—women, the elderly, and children.

Those conquered people who were captured but not killed during the Roman invasions were kept as slaves. The Roman Empire's economy depended on slaves to plant and harvest crops for its vast territories and to work producing things like jugs and other pottery. Those who had not fought and who lived in small villages like Nazareth were left to plant their fields and work at the crafts they were trained for. The one big change was that now they had to accumulate money in the form of coins to pay taxes to Rome and temple fees to the Jewish hierarchy in Jerusalem. For hundreds of years before this, a farmer paid a

An antique print of Roman soldiers in battle gear. [North Wind Picture Archives]

portion of his crop as a tax to his rulers. He bartered food for services such as the repair of his roof, or goods such as a baby goat. Now the economy of Judea and Galilee had changed. The taxes and fees were so steep that some people had to exchange all their crops for coins and did not have enough food to feed themselves. Most people suffered quietly. A few brave—or foolhardy—ones spoke out.

Under Roman rule, a rebellious person or tax avoider was often made an example of, sometimes given the ultimate punishment: crucifixion. Judas of Gamala was one such rebel. Judas was a learned man, and a husband and father, who longed to raise his children in a better world—a Galilee ruled by faithful Jews instead of the Roman puppets who crippled Judas and his people with unbearable taxes. Judas traveled through the farming villages and fishing ports of Galilee, preaching a message of revolt to the impoverished peasants, urging them not to pay taxes to Rome or give a portion of their earnings to the temple in Jerusalem. He compared the taxation to a form of slavery and encouraged his fellow Jews to rise up against their oppressors. And he said that bowing down to Augustus Caesar and Rome instead of the one true God was sinful. The Romans might have overlooked Judas as a religious nut, if he had not raised an army of peasants to attempt a violent overthrow of the Roman-sponsored government in Galilee. That action brought an immediate response: Judas of Gamala must die.

By order of Herod Antipas, the tetrarch or administrator of Galilee working for the Romans, soldiers captured Judas and began the crucifixion process. To discourage other dissenters, a crowd was encouraged to watch the agony of Judas. Jesus and many other Galileans bore witness to the horror.

✦ ✦ ✦ ✦ ✦

The soldiers of Antipas strip Judas of Gamala naked in the palace courtyard. They force him to his knees, facing a low post. He is tied to it with his hands above his head. Two soldiers pick up short-handled whips, whose leather lashes are tipped with lead balls and mutton bones. The soldiers stand ready to take turns striking Judas across his back, leaning into each blow with all their strength. As each lash is inflicted, the leather thongs tear open the skin and muscles, even as the lead and bone create deep bruising.

Judas cries out in agony as a soldier delivers another blast of leather onto his flesh. But he knows better than to curse his executioners, because that will only mean more blows. So he endures the torture. In moments, Judas is covered with blood.

As with all aspects of Roman execution, the stripping and lashing has a specific purpose: the public nudity humiliates, while the whip breaks Judas's will so that he will offer no resistance when nailed to the cross. Crucifixion, Roman-style, is not just a barbarous way to kill, but also a process of mentally and physically destroying the victim—whether it be man, woman, or child. Judas will be nothing but an empty husk by the time he hangs from the cross.

Judas of Gamala lies limp and bleeding after the whipping. Soldiers then bring out a rough-hewn piece of lumber and hurl it to the ground. Despite the blood pouring down his back, Judas is forced to stand. His executioners lift this splinter-filled board onto his shoulders. This will become the crossbar of his crucifix, and like all condemned men, Judas has to carry it outside the city walls to a spot where a vertical pole in the ground will form the second part. He will be nailed to that cross and left to die. His legs will be broken to make the torturous process even more ghastly. He will hang in full view of thousands. Judas will be dead by nightfall—if he is lucky.

The story of Judas's execution will be shared among the Jews of Galilee. But he is not alone. There are countless other would-be prophets who think violence can bring an end to Roman occupation. They will all pay for this conceit with their lives.

+ + + + +

The Jews were a conquered people when Jesus was born. Although the Roman emperor had instructed his representatives to respect and not interfere with their religious traditions, all other aspects of their daily lives were under his control.

What gave them the strength to endure hardship and humiliation under Roman rule was the knowledge that they were a chosen people.

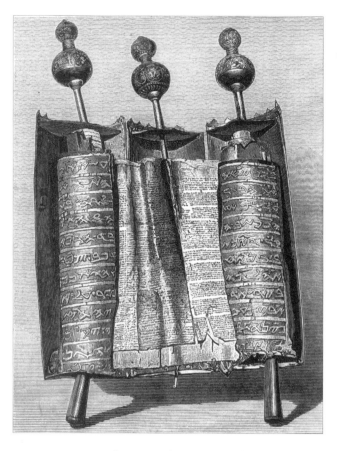

Engraving printed in 1878 of an ancient Palestinian scroll of the Torah. [Mary Evans Picture Library]

In the Torah, the holy book of Jewish scripture, Moses says, "For you are a people holy to the Lord your God. The Lord your God has chosen you out of all the peoples on the face of the earth to be his people, his treasured possession." This chosenness was matched with the promise from God that he would send a savior to free the people.

As the Jewish people waited for their savior and king, they maintained their faith in one God among the Romans, who believed in multiple gods and even that their emperor was a god. The Jewish people listened to preachers who traveled the lands speaking of prophecies soon to be fulfilled. And they journeyed each year to their birthplace for the census count, so the Roman emperor would know exactly how much money he would make from the people of Judea and Galilee.

Marble sculpture of Moses by Michelangelo made between 1513 and 1516 for the tomb of Pope Julius II in Rome. [The Bridgeman Art Library]

✦ BOOK I ✦

YOUNG JESUS of NAZARETH

Ci apres commence le .xv. liure
des anciennetes des uifs selond
la sentence de ioseph.

[Q]uand herodes eut prin
se la principaute de
toute iudee to' ceulx
qui troiuia priues
et fauourables il

cleua a grans dignites mais ceu
qui sentoyent ou faisoyent du cō
traire il ne cessoit tous les iours
de mettre a griefs tourmens. Et
sur tous les aultres estoient hon
noures enuers li phion le phari
seen et samee son disciple. Car qn
les therosolimites furent assied

CHAPTER 1

THE MASSACRE IN BETHLEHEM

MARCH, 5 BC ✦ BETHLEHEM, JUDEA

JOSEPH AND MARY AND THEIR INFANT SON, JESUS, barely get out of Bethlehem alive. Joseph awakes from a terrifying dream and has a vision of what is to come. He rouses Mary and Jesus, and they escape into the night.

Now soldiers are walking toward Bethlehem. They have come from the capital city of Jerusalem and are approaching this small town, intent on finding and killing a baby boy. The child's name, unknown to them, is Jesus, and his only crime is that some believe he will be the next king of the Jewish people. The current ruler of the land, a tyrant named Herod the Great, is determined to ensure the baby's death. None of the soldiers know what the child's mother and father look like or the precise location of his home, so they plan to kill every baby boy in

Capture of Jerusalem by Herod in 36 BC. *An illustration from a 1470 French translation of Flavius Josephus's* Antiquities of the Jews. [The Bridgeman Art Library]

Bethlehem and the surrounding area. This alone will guarantee that the threat is eliminated.

Herod first learns about Jesus from travelers who have come to worship the baby. These men, called Magi, are astronomers and wise men who study the world's great religious texts. Among these books is the Tanakh, a collection of history, prophecy, poetry, and songs telling the story of the Jewish people. The wealthy foreigners travel almost a thousand miles over rugged desert, following an extraordinarily bright star that shines in the sky each morning before dawn. "Where is the one who has been born king of the Jews?" they ask on their arrival in Herod's court. "We saw his star when it rose and have come to worship him."

Amazingly, the Magi carry treasure chests filled with gold, as well as the sweet-smelling tree resins myrrh and frankincense. These are learned, studious men. Herod can only conclude that the Magi are either foolhardy for risking the theft of such a great fortune by carrying it across the vast desert to get to Jerusalem, or that they truly believe this child will be the new king.

After the Magi ask their question, a furious Herod summons his religious advisers. He insists that these teachers of religious law and temple high priests tell him exactly where to find this new king.

The teachers whom Herod first interrogates are humble men. They wear simple white linen caps and robes. Then he moves on to the bearded temple high priests. They dress elaborately, in white

The wealthy foreigners travel more than a thousand miles over rugged desert.

and blue linen caps and turbans with gold bands on the brows, and blue robes adorned in bright tassels and bells. Over this they wear capes and purses decorated with gold and precious stones. Their clothing signifies their stature as high-level temple leaders. Herod demands of the teachers and priests, "Where is this so-called king of the Jews?"

"Bethlehem, in the land of Judah." They quote verbatim from the prophet Micah, whose words are recorded in the Tanakh. Some seven centuries earlier, Micah said that the person who would save the Jewish people would be born in Bethlehem. "Out of you [Bethlehem] will come . . . one who will be ruler over Israel. . . ."

Herod sends the Magi on their way. His parting royal instruction is that they locate the infant, then return to Jerusalem and tell Herod the child's precise location so that he can visit this new king himself.

The Magi see through this deceit. They never go back to Jerusalem.

An illustration of frankincense from a book on medicinal plants published in 1887. The resin from this tree was used to make incense and perfume.
[The Bridgeman Art Library]

✦　✦　✦　✦　✦

For centuries, Jewish prophets have predicted the coming of a new king to rule their people. They have prophesied five specific occurrences that would take place to confirm the Messiah's birth.

The first is that a great star will rise in the east.

The second is that the baby will be born in Bethlehem, the small town where the great King David was born a thousand years ago.

The third prophecy is that the child will also be a direct

descendant of David, a fact that can easily be confirmed by the temple's meticulous genealogical records.

Fourth, powerful men will travel from afar to worship him.

And finally, the child's mother will be a virgin.

What troubles Herod most deeply is knowing that three of these events have occurred. He would be even more distressed to learn that the remaining two are also true. The child is from the line of David, and his teenage mother, Mary, attests that she is a virgin, despite her pregnancy.

Herod gazes out of his palace window, waiting to hear that all the baby boys in Bethlehem have been killed. He is afraid of what will happen if a king rises up to save the Jewish people. One result is likely: it will mean the end of his good life. Even though he is half Jewish, Herod's allegiance is to Rome.

Judea is part, though only a small part, of the vast Roman Empire—a sprawling kingdom stretching the length of Europe, across Asia Minor, and including almost the entire Mediterranean rim. But Herod's kingdom is different from any other under Rome's iron fist: it is the only Jewish territory. The Jewish people are an ancient civilization founded on a belief system that is at odds with Rome's. The Jewish people believe in one true God; the rest of the empire worships many pagan deities and even considers its emperor divine. Herod stands between the Jews and the Roman emperor Augustus Caesar in their uneasy relationship. Rome will leave the Jews alone as long as Herod keeps his people productive so they can pay the high taxes that Rome demands.

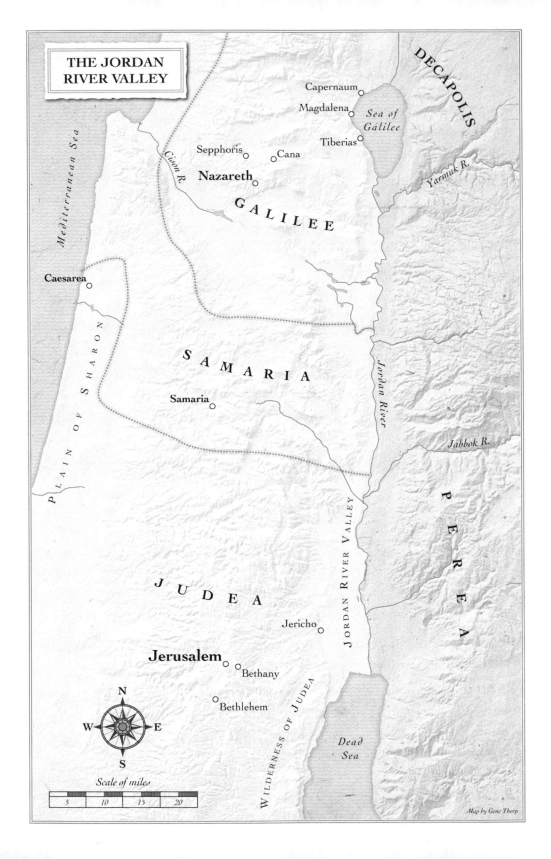

THE JORDAN
RIVER VALLEY

Mediterranean Sea

Cison R.

DECAPOLIS

Capernaum ○
Magdalena ○   *Sea of
Galilee*
Tiberias ○

Sepphoris ○   Cana ○

Nazareth ○

G A L I L E E

Yarmuk R.

Caesarea ○

S A M A R I A

Jordan River

P L A I N   O F   S H A R O N

Samaria ○

Jabbok R.

P
E
R
E
A

J U D E A

Jericho ○

J O R D A N   R I V E R   V A L L E Y

Jerusalem ○ ○ Bethany

Bethlehem ○

N
W   E
S

*Dead
Sea*

W I L D E R N E S S   O F   J U D E A

Scale of miles

| 5 | 10 | 15 | 20 |

Map by Gene Thorp

✦ ✦ ✦ ✦ ✦

Herod doesn't know it, but Jesus and his parents have already traveled to Jerusalem twice before to pay visits to the great temple, the most important and sacred building in all Judea. Perched atop a massive stone platform that gives it the appearance of a fortress rather than a place of worship, the temple is a physical embodiment of the Jewish people and their ancient faith. The temple was first built by Solomon in the tenth century BC. It was leveled by the Babylonians in 586 BC and then rebuilt nearly fifty years later. Herod recently renovated the entire complex and increased the temple's size. Now it is not just a symbol of Judaism, but of the king himself.

Eight days after Jesus's birth, his parents made their first visit to the temple so that he might be circumcised. There the child was formally named Jesus. The second visit came when he was forty days old. The baby boy was brought to the temple and presented to God, in keeping with the laws of the Jewish faith. His father, Joseph, a carpenter, dutifully purchased a pair of young turtledoves to be sacrificed in honor of this solemn occasion.

Something very strange occurred as Jesus and his parents entered the temple on that day, something that hinted he might truly be a very special child. Mary, Joseph, and Jesus were traveling quietly, not doing anything that would draw attention. Even so, two complete strangers—an old man and an old woman, both of whom

[NEXT PAGES] *Jerusalem as an artist imagined it may have looked in AD 65, drawn in 1887.* [Mary Evans Picture Library]

A. MOUNT MORIAH.

B. MOUNT ZION.

1.1.1 Mount of Olives.

2 Road to Bethany.

3 Place where Jesus wept.

4 Garden of Gethsemane.

5.5.5 Valley of Jehoshaphat.

6.6 Brook Kedron.

7 Point of Ascension.

8 Absalom's Pillar.

9 The Village of Siloam.

10 Hill of Offence.

11 Hill of Evil Council.

12 House of Caiaphas.

13 Aaceldama, or Field of Blood.

14 The Temple.

15 Golden Gate.

16 Porch of Solomon.

17.17 Pool of Bethesda.

18 Acqueduct.

19 Road to Bethlehem.

20.20 Tower of Antonia.

21.21 Via Dolorosa.

22 Fish Market.

23 St. Stephen's Gate.

24 Fish Gate.

25 Old Gate.

26 Gate of Ephrem.

27 Gate of Herod.

28 Hebron Gate.

29 Gate of Esseans.

30 Zion Gate.

ANCIENT

A.D.

JERUSALEM

65

C. UPPER CITY.	D BEZETHA.	
31 Sheep Market.	41 The Lower Court.	51 Great Market.
32 Tower of Acra.	42 Upper Court.	52 Dung Gate.
33 Tower of Hippicus.	43 Hall of Judgment.	53 Palace of the Kings.
34 Calvary.	44 Pilate's House.	54 Circus.
35 Holy Sepulchre.	45 Tyropean Valley.	55 Theatre.
36 Pool of Hezekiah.	46 High Bridge	56.56.56 Valley of Ghion.
37 Palace of Helena.	47 Solomon's Gate.	57 Upper Pool of Ghion.
38 Tower of Psephnia.	48 Hippodrome.	58 Road to Joppa.
39 Judgment Gate.	49 Xystus.	59 Wilderness of St. John.
40 Tower of Phasœlus.	50 Prison.	60 Bethlehem.

knew nothing about this baby called Jesus or his fulfillment of the prophecy—saw him from across the crowded temple and came to him.

The approaching old man's name was Simeon, and he was of the belief that he would not die until he laid eyes upon the new king of the Jews. Simeon asked if he might hold the baby. Mary and Joseph agreed. As Simeon took Jesus into his arms, he offered a prayer to God, thanking him for the chance to see this new king with his own eyes. Then Simeon handed Jesus back to Mary with these words: "This child is destined to cause the falling and rising of many in Israel, and to be a sign that will be spoken against, so that the thoughts of many hearts will be revealed. And a sword will pierce your own soul too."

At that very moment, a woman named Anna approached. She was an eighty-four-year-old widowed prophetess, who spent her waking hours in the temple, fasting and praying. Simeon's words were still ringing in Mary's and Joseph's ears as Anna stepped forward and also praised Jesus. She loudly thanked God for bringing this special baby boy into the world. Then she made a most unusual claim, predicting to Mary and Joseph that their son would free Jerusalem from Roman rule.

Mary and Joseph marveled at Simeon's and Anna's words, flattered for the attention, as all new parents would be, but also unsure what this talk about swords and redemption truly meant. They finished their business and departed into the bustling city of

Jerusalem, both elated and fearful for the life their son might be destined to lead.

✦ ✦ ✦ ✦ ✦

There are many more prophecies about the life of Jesus outlined in Scripture. Slowly but surely, as this child grows to manhood, those predictions will also come true. Jesus's behavior will brand him as a revolutionary, known throughout Judea for his startling speeches and teachings. He will be adored by the Jewish people but become a threat to those who profit from the populace: the high priests, the temple elders, the puppet rulers of Judea, and most of all, the Roman Empire.

And Rome does not tolerate a threat. The Romans have learned and mastered the arts of torture and persecution. Revolutionaries and troublemakers are dealt with in harsh and horrific fashion in order that others won't be tempted to copy their ways.

So it will be with Jesus. This, too, will fulfill prophecy.

All of that is to come. For now Jesus is still an infant, cared for and loved by Mary and Joseph. He was born in a stable, visited by the Magi, presented with their lavish gifts, and is now being pursued by Herod and the Roman Empire.

And it is Joseph who will train the boy to be obedient and strong, to follow Jewish ways and obey Jewish laws.

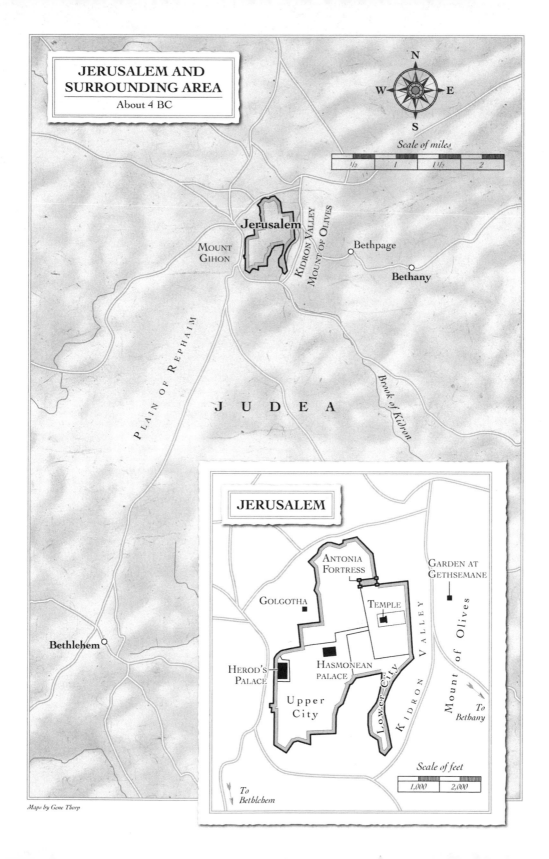

JERUSALEM AND SURROUNDING AREA
About 4 BC

N
W   E
S

Scale of miles

1/2   1   1 1/2   2

Jerusalem

MOUNT GIHON

KIDRON VALLEY

MOUNT OF OLIVES

Bethpage

Bethany

PLAIN OF REPHAIM

Brook of Kidron

J U D E A

Bethlehem

JERUSALEM

ANTONIA FORTRESS

GARDEN AT GETHSEMANE

GOLGOTHA

TEMPLE

HEROD'S PALACE

HASMONEAN PALACE

Upper City

Lower City

KIDRON VALLEY

Mount of Olives

To Bethany

To Bethlehem

Scale of feet

1,000   2,000

Maps by Gene Thorp

CHAPTER 2

GROWING UP IN NAZARETH

5 BC–AD 7 ✦ NAZARETH

Jesus spends his youth and young adulthood in the village of Nazareth in the region of Galilee. His father, Joseph, is a tradesman, building with stone and making furniture with wood.

Joseph is a direct descendant of Abraham, the patriarch of the Jewish faith, and David, the greatest king Judea has ever known. Twenty-seven generations separate Joseph

from Abraham, and at least fifteen separate him from David. But while Abraham was extremely wealthy, and David and his son Solomon even more so, their lineage has fallen on hard times. The quiet and humble backdrop of Nazareth is a far cry from the great kingdoms enjoyed by those prior generations. It is a village of less than four hundred residents situated in a hollow between the rolling hills of southern Galilee. The roads are unpaved, and the village is not protected from invaders by walls or other fortifications. An ancient caravan route passes within six miles, but no major highways go directly through Nazareth. It is a small town that is destined to remain that way, thanks not just to its location, but also to the fact that the sole water source is a single spring that can support only a small number of people.

Various families share dwellings, sometimes separated by small courtyards. The tiny houses are built from the soft limestone and other rocks that litter the nearby hills.

The typical home in Nazareth is one or two stories, built into the side of the hills. The floors are made of dirt tamped down with ash and clay, while the walls are made of stone. Mud is smeared in the joints between the stones to keep out the wind and rain. The roof is flat, made of wood, straw, mud, and lime. The bottom floor is reserved for storage, housing for the animals at night, and a cooking fire, while the upper floor is used for sleeping on thin mattresses stuffed with wool. A ladder leads from one floor to the other. There are no indoor bathing or bathroom facilities.

Mary is in charge of the home, feeding and clothing her family. She grinds barley and wheat into flour, cards wool from sheep and spins it into thread to weave cloth, carries water from the well in a large jar every day for washing and cooking.

When the rains come on time, the hills around Nazareth produce ample crops for meals: beans, vegetables, fruits such as grapes and pomegranates, and nuts. Mary feeds the chickens, collects eggs, and takes care of the family donkey. And in a village where people are close and supportive, she will watch other women's children, take care of the sick and elderly, and share any surplus her family has with others less fortunate.

As a builder, Joseph works with both foundation stone and oak from nearby forests to construct buildings and furniture. When work is scarce in Nazareth, there are always jobs to be found in the city of Sepphoris, just an hour's walk away.

Like his father before him, Joseph trains his son to follow in his craft, teaching the boy not only how to build, but also other vital skills such as pressing grapes to make wine, and olives to make olive oil; terracing a hillside to grow the crops that will feed the family; and rerouting the local spring for irrigation. But most important of

A modern photograph of the remains of an olive press. The beam, weighed down by stones, crushed the olives in the baskets. The olive juice that was squeezed out collected in the carved trough and dripped through the hole into storage cisterns that were buried in the ground. [Kurt Prescott]

סדר
תפלות לערב עם
שמנה עשרה וברכת
המזון וקריחת שמע
וקידוש של שבת וי"ט
עם ברכת הנהנין
ויתפלת הדרך
נכתב ביום ה' ו' כסליו
תקל"ד
לפ"ק
בפיורדא
ויחל משה
הצילני נא

all, Joseph raises Jesus in the Jewish faith. For though the Greek, Arab, and Roman cultures have all made their marks on Nazareth over the centuries, those in Joseph's lineage have not changed in their devotion to the one true God. It has been the core of their belief since Abraham walked the earth two thousand years before.

Nazareth is a wonderful place for a young boy to grow up. There are hills to climb, caves to explore, and fields through which to run. In the summer, when the air is so hot that Jesus sleeps on the flat roof of the family home, it is time to harvest figs and olives. Spring is a time for planting the wheat that will provide their daily bread. Nazareth is only twenty miles from the Mediterranean Sea, but it might as well be a thousand, because fish is almost as rare as red meat in young Jesus's diet. So while it is not a life of excess, there is always enough: the trees and fields produce olives, wheat, onions, and lentils; there is an occasional piece of lamb and eggs that can be cooked in that most precious of all staples, olive oil. The oil is also used for fueling lamps and rubbing into chapped skin.

Mary and Joseph are devout and have gone to great lengths to pass their faith on to Jesus. A small wooden box containing a parchment scroll hangs on their doorpost. On it is written the Shema, that most elemental of Jewish prayers: "Hear, O Israel, the Lord our God, the Lord is One." It is a prayer that the family recites on rising in the morning and after bringing the animals into the house at

Text of the Shema, the Hebrew prayer that is the centerpiece of Jewish morning and evening prayers. An 18th-century watercolor on paper. [The Bridgeman Art Library]

bedtime each night. Jesus's clothing is adorned with tassels, in accordance with the writings in Deuteronomy, the fifth book of the Hebrew Scripture, and he attends synagogue every week. There, in the small square room, Jesus wears a prayer shawl while sitting on a bench with his back against the wall, reading from the sacred scrolls and singing the psalms. It is in the synagogue that he learns to read and write, because during this time of Roman occupation, holding on to tradition has become a priority for the Jewish people. A group of pious teachers known as the Pharisees helps support schools in synagogues that teach children Hebrew and instruct them in the Jewish law.

CHAPTER 3

ARCHELAUS, HEIR OF HEROD THE GREAT

4 BC–AD 6 ✦ JERUSALEM

KING HEROD THE GREAT IS DEAD. HE DIED SHORTLY after the massacre of male babies in Bethlehem, without knowing whether he had succeeded in killing the infant king of the Jews. But the Jewish people are no better off. Rioting takes place in Jerusalem when it becomes clear that Herod's heir, his son Archelaus, is just like his father. He shows that he can be as cruel as Herod the Great.

It happens during Passover, the celebration that symbolizes the freedom from slavery achieved when Moses led the people out of Egypt in search of the homeland God had promised them.

Passover is a time when Jerusalem is packed with hundreds of thousands of worshippers from all over the world, so it is a shock when Archelaus boldly asserts his authority by ordering his cavalry to charge their horses into the thick crowds filling the

Passover Customs in the First Century AD

Passover, the festival of celebration, was and still is one of the most important times of the year for people of the Jewish faith. It recalls the time when the Israelites, ancestors of the Jews, were captives in Egypt. God sent Moses to the Egyptian pharaoh with the demand that the pharaoh release his people. When the pharaoh refused, God sent plagues and other torments to the land. Finally, God killed all the first-born sons of Egypt, but "passed over" Jewish households. Pharaoh was defeated; he released Moses and his people that day. The story is that the people had to leave so quickly that they could not wait for their bread dough to rise and so packed it flat and unrisen. That is why unleavened bread is eaten during Passover.

During Jesus's lifetime, this is what might have happened in a household as Passover approached and at the meal.

These customs were maintained even if a family traveled to Jerusalem and stayed with friends or camped on the hillsides surrounding the city.

- Selection or purchase of an animal for sacrifice

- Searching the home, courtyards, and campsites for leaven, any food that has been made with yeast

- Foot washing, performed by a servant or slave for anyone who visited the family

The Passover meal might consist of olives or pickled vegetables, roast lamb, unleavened bread, and wine. The head of the family and the guests would have parts of Scripture to read and responses to make, and children would be assigned questions to elicit answers telling the story of the original Passover.

DE ANTIQVITATIBVS LIBER OCTAVVSDECIMVS INCIPIT. QVI CONTINZ
TEMPVS ANNORVM TRIGINTA TRIVM

ualiter cyrinus a cesare ad syriam censandam destinatus cum cop…io iudeos
substantias depreciaturus et archelao pecunias redditurus in iudeam ueniens. per
suadente iozaro pontifice a iudeis permittitur. Capitulum Primum.

YRINVS AVTEM VNVS DE HIS qui
semper in consultatione congregabantur: uir per
omnium magisteriorum & principiorum officia ce
lebratus per cunctas aministrationes ad consulat
culmen ascendens: & in cunctis alns dignitatibus
clarus cum paucis uenit ad syriam. censor gentis
a cesare destinatus: & approbator uniuscuiusque
sententie. Mittitur etiam cum eo copinus ductor
totius equestris agminis potestatemq; iudeorum omnium ferens. Venit etia
cyrinus iudeam nam dispensationi syrie fuerat adunata uniuersorum de

temple courts. Wielding javelins and long, straight steel and bronze swords, Archelaus's soldiers massacre three thousand innocent pilgrims. Mary, Joseph, and Jesus see the bloodbath firsthand and are lucky to escape with their lives. They are also eyewitnesses to the crucifixion of more than two thousand Jewish rebels outside Jerusalem's city walls when Roman soldiers move in to quell further riots. The horrible deaths are examples of what happens to those who defy the Roman Empire.

Engraving of the Great Sanhedrin, the high court of the Jews of Jerusalem; no date. [Mary Evans Picture Library]

[LEFT] *An illustration of Caesar sending Senator Cyrenius to collect taxes in Syria and Judea. From a 1503 edition of a 4th-century Latin translation of Flavius Josephus's* Antiquities of the Jews. [The Bridgeman Art Library]

Rome soon inserts itself completely into Judean politics. In AD 6, Augustus Caesar deems Archelaus unfit to rule and exiles him to Gaul. Herod's fifth son, Antipas, takes the reins with the title of tetrarch.

The city of Jerusalem is controlled by the local aristocracy and temple high priests, who mete out justice through the Great Sanhedrin, a court composed of seventy-one judges with absolute authority to enforce Jewish religious law. People involved in religious disputes must travel to Jerusalem to present their cases. The Sanhedrin determine all punishments except the death sentence; that must get the approval of the Roman governor.

By letting the Jewish hierarchy rule Jerusalem, Augustus Caesar balances the needs of his empire without insulting the Jewish faith. Nevertheless, he still demands complete submission, a humiliation that the Jews have no choice but to endure. This does not mean, however, that they have stopped rebelling. In fact, their region is the site of more uprisings than any other part of the mighty Roman Empire.

The Jewish people begin boycotting the purchase of all Roman pottery. As passive and understated as that act may be, it serves as a daily reminder that despite their oppression, the Jews will never allow themselves to be completely trampled beneath the heel of Rome.

Caesar Augustus, first emperor of the Roman Empire. An illustration from Crabb's Historical Dictionary, *1835.* [Universal Images Group/SuperStock]

CHAPTER 4

MISSING

MARCH 22, AD 7 ✦ JORDAN RIVER VALLEY, JUDEA

JESUS IS MISSING.

Mary and Joseph don't realize it yet as they walk in the long line of pilgrims on their way back to Nazareth after the Passover festival in Jerusalem. They are required by Jewish law to make this journey each year. Leaving the city, thousands of worshippers have been stopped at the gate to pay yet another one of the high taxes that make their lives such a struggle—this time a tariff on goods purchased in Jerusalem. Now they are headed home to Galilee. The pilgrims march in an enormous caravan to ensure protection from robbers, kidnappers, and slavers. Mary and Joseph's fellow travelers are hardly strangers, for they make this journey together each year. The members of the caravan look after one another and their families. If a child has

Modern photograph of a gate in the Old City walls in Jerusalem.
[The Bridgeman Art Library]

wandered away from his parents at nightfall, he is given a place to sleep and then sent off to find his parents in the morning.

Mary and Joseph believe this is what has become of Jesus. He is a bright and charismatic child who gets along well with others, so it was no surprise when he failed to sit with them at the campfire last night. They fully trusted that he would turn up in the morning.

But now morning has come and gone. And as the noontime sun looms high overhead, Mary and Joseph realize that it has been a very long time since they've seen their son. They walk the length of the caravan in search of their lost boy, growing more and more concerned, pleading with fellow pilgrims for some clue as to his whereabouts. But not a single person can remember seeing Jesus since leaving Jerusalem.

Mary and Joseph realize that they have not only lost their child, but in all probability, they have left him behind.

With no choice, they turn around and march back up the road. They will walk alone all the way to Jerusalem. Nothing matters more than finding Jesus.

CHAPTER 5

JESUS SITS WITH THE RABBIS

MARCH 23, AD 7 ✦ JERUSALEM

MARY AND JOSEPH FINALLY ARRIVE BACK IN JERUSALEM. Now, somewhere among the crowds and soldiers and exotic travelers in this crowded, fast-paced city, they must find him.

Meanwhile, the Son of God, as Jesus will refer to himself for the first time on this very day, is sitting in the temple and listening with rapt fascination as a group of Jewish scholars share insights about their common faith. Now that the thousands of Passover pilgrims have gone, the worshippers in this most holy building have resumed their normal routines of prayer, fasting, worship, sacrifice, and teaching. It is a rhythm the child has never before experienced, and he enjoys it immensely. If anyone thinks it odd that a twelve-year-old, smooth-cheeked, simply dressed child from rural Galilee should be sitting alone among these gray-bearded rabbis, with their flowing robes and encyclopedic knowledge of Jewish history, they do not say. In fact, the opposite is true: Jesus's understanding of complex spiritual concepts has astonished the priests and teachers. They marvel to one another about his amazing gifts.

Jesus is quite aware that his parents have already begun the journey home to Nazareth. He is not an insensitive child, but his thirst for knowledge and eagerness to share his own insights is so great that it never crosses his mind that Mary and Joseph will be worried about him. Nor does Jesus believe that his actions mean he is being disobedient. The need to dig deeper into the meaning of God overwhelms every other consideration. Like all Jewish boys, when he begins puberty, he will go from being considered a mere boy to being thought of as a full-fledged member of the religious community and thus accountable for his actions. But Jesus is different from other boys his age. He is not content to merely learn the oral history of his faith, but also feels a keen desire to debate its fine points. So deep is this need that even now, three days since his parents departed for home, Jesus is still finding new questions to ask.

✦   ✦   ✦   ✦   ✦

Mary and Joseph enter the temple complex through the southern doors and then climb the broad stone staircase leading up onto the Temple Mount. They find themselves standing on a large and crowded plaza, where they begin scanning the many worshippers, searching for their lost son.

It is almost impossible to know where to look first. The temple is a three-acre platform with walls stretching a quarter-mile in length and looming 450 feet over the Kidron Valley below. The majority of the Mount is the vast open-air stone courtyard where they now stand. It is known as the Court of the Gentiles and is open to both Jew and Gentile (non-Jew).

Seeing no sign of Jesus, they move to the center of the Mount. There, like a fifteen-story limestone and gold island, rises the temple. This is not merely a place of worship, but a refuge from the repression of Roman occupation, a place where all Jews can speak freely and pray to God without fear. There are separate courtyards

The Temple Mount

The temple in Jerusalem was the center of Jewish life throughout the world. Jews living as far away as Gaul, in what is now western Europe, traveled to the temple especially for the three major festivals: Passover (in Hebrew, *Pesach*), Sukkoth, and Shabuoth. The temple was built on Mount Moriah, the place where God is thought to have gathered the dust to make Adam, and where Abraham brought his son Isaac to be sacrificed when God tested his faith. (Abraham passed his test because he was willing to sacrifice his son. God allowed Isaac to live.) The First Temple was built by Solomon and destroyed by Nebuchadnezzar. The Second Temple was built between 538 BC and 516 BC. In the Roman era, Herod the Great decided to expand the temple, a task that took more than ten thousand workers. Finished in 19 BC, the renovated complex now spread over thirty-six acres. The temple itself and its courts sit in one corner at an immense plaza. It is said that one million pilgrims could fit in the Temple Mount.

Pilgrims came to the temple on holy days, but also to pray during services, to study the Torah with one of the many teachers there, to ask questions of the scholars, and to make offerings to God.

The whole structure is known as the Temple Mount, because it was built on a mountain. The complex encloses a series of courtyards decreasing in size and increasing in importance until one reaches the temple itself.

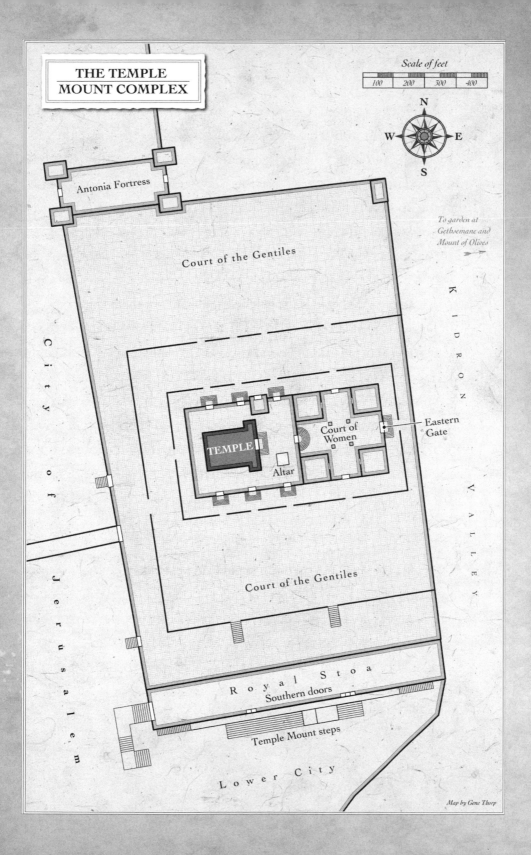

for men and women, rooms for priests to sleep in when they are not on duty, stairs and terraces from which those priests teach the Jewish faith, and altars where sheep, doves, and young cows are sacrificed. The temple is the first thing visitors to Jerusalem see as they come up over the surrounding hills and gaze down on the city.

It is surrounded on four sides by a low wall that separates it from the Court of the Gentiles. Only Jews can cross from one side of the wall to the other. Just in case a Roman soldier or other Gentile is tempted to step through the gates, a sign reminds them that they will be killed. "Foreigners!" reads the inscription. "Do not enter within the grille and partition surrounding the temple. He who is caught will only have himself to blame for his death which will follow."

The words are a reminder that this is a holy place. According to tradition, this is the precise location atop Mount Moriah where Abraham almost sacrificed Isaac, where King David chose to build the First Temple, and where God gathered dust to create Adam, the first man. There is no more profound or greater symbol of Jewish belief.

✦　✦　✦　✦　✦

Mary and Joseph step through the temple gate, leaving the Court of Gentiles behind. Now their task gets even more frustrating, because Jesus could be inside any of the many rooms within the temple—or in none. They scour the place with the same frantic urgency with which they searched the bazaars and alleys of Jerusalem earlier in the day.

As Mary and Joseph make their way through the courts, the

[ABOVE] *A woodcut of King David playing a harp; no date.* [North Wind Picture Archives]

[RIGHT] *A 12th-century stone carving of King David.* [The Bridgeman Art Library]

sounds and smells of cows and sheep fill the air as priests prepare the animals for their ceremonial deaths on the altar and clean up the gallons of blood that flow when an animal is offered up to God. Ritual animal sacrifices are a constant of temple life. An animal is slaughtered as a symbol that an individual's sins are forgiven.

Finally, outside on the terrace where the sages and scribes teach the Scriptures to believers during Passover and other feasts, Mary hears Jesus's voice. But the words coming from his mouth sound nothing like those of the son she knows so well. Jesus has never shown any sign of such deep knowledge of Jewish law and tradition. Mary and Joseph gasp in shock at the ease with which he discusses God.

Nevertheless, they are also understandably irate. "Son," Mary interrupts, "why have you treated us like this? Your father and I have been anxiously searching for you."

"Why were you searching for me?" he responds. There is innocence to his words. "Didn't you know I had to be in my Father's house?"

If the esteemed temple rabbis overhear Jesus's response, they don't let on. For if the boy is suggesting that God is his actual father—literally, and not just figuratively—then what he says is a claim of divinity and would be blasphemy. His punishment would be death by stoning. Jewish law says that on commitment of blasphemy, the entire congregation should place their hands upon the blasphemer, then step back and hurl rocks at his defenseless head and body until he collapses and dies.

Distant view of Jerusalem. An engraving made in 1846. [Mary Evans Picture Library]

But under the law, Jesus cannot be convicted of blasphemy because he is only twelve. He has not come of age and is not yet responsible for his words. So perhaps the rabbis do hear his bold statement and breathe a sigh of relief, knowing that this brilliant young scholar is exempt from a most cruel death.

Jesus rises from among the rabbis. He goes to Mary and Joseph, and together they begin the long walk back to Nazareth.

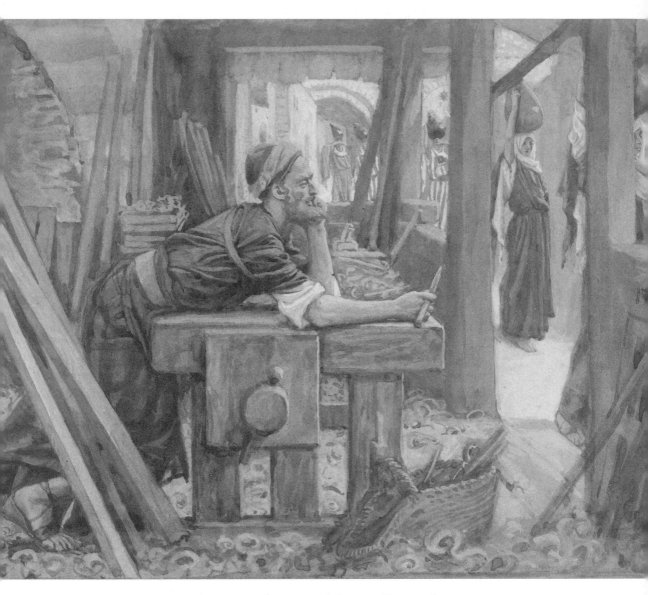

The Anxiety of Saint Joseph *by James Tissot, 19th century.*
Watercolor over graphite on paper. [The Bridgeman Art Library]

CHAPTER 6

THE CARPENTER

AD 7–25 ✦ NAZARETH AND SEPPHORIS

T HERE IS NOTHING EXCEPTIONAL ABOUT JESUS'S upbringing. He labors six days a week as a tradesman alongside his father, building the roofs and doorposts of Nazareth and laying the foundation stones of nearby sprawling Sepphoris. Any other young man would be destined to remain here always, raising a family and building his own home into the slope of a Nazarene hill.

But the young Jesus has another destiny. The holiness and magnificence of Jerusalem call to him. He comes to know the smells and music of the city during his annual Passover visits, even as he becomes comfortable navigating his way through such local landmarks as the Mount of Olives, the garden at Gethsemane, the Kidron Valley, and the temple itself. With every passing year, as Jesus grows from a child into a man with a carpenter's square shoulders and callused hands, his

Salomé

Hérode

wisdom and awareness of his faith increase. He develops the gifts of serenity and powerful personal charisma, and learns to speak eloquently in public.

Yet Jesus is cautious when he talks to crowds. Accountable for his behavior as a full-fledged member of the Jewish religious community now, he knows that blasphemous talk about being the Son of God will lead to a public execution. Either his fellow Jews would stone him for such language or the Romans might kill him for suggesting he is their divine emperor's equal. Stoning would seem a tame way to die in comparison with the tortures of which the Romans are capable.

The most common methods of killing a condemned man in the Roman Empire are hanging, burning him alive, beheading, placing him inside a bag full of scorpions then drowning him, and crucifixion. As terrible as the first four might be, the last is considered the worst by far. Even though crucifixion is practiced regularly throughout the Roman Empire, it is a death so horrible that it is forbidden to execute Roman citizens in this manner. But people in Judea are not considered Roman citizens. And their new ruler, Herod the Great's fifth son, Herod Antipas, uses this cruel punishment freely.

Joseph and Mary live in fear of Herod Antipas, as do other Jews. With a dark beard covering the tip of his chin and a thin mustache, he even looks the part of a true villain. He was born in Judea but educated in Rome, a city that he adores. He pays homage

Sketch of Herod Antipas created for a modern opera about Salome. [DeAgostini/ Getty Images]

to Augustus Caesar and Rome by heavily taxing the Jews in his power, and he enjoys ordering Roman-style forms of execution for anyone who dares defy him.

Outrage against Rome has been building for decades. The people of Galilee have been levied with tax after tax after tax. Herod Antipas is a lover of luxury, and he uses some of these taxes to rebuild Sepphoris and finance his own lavish lifestyle. The more luxury Herod wants, the higher the taxes climb.

Actual money is scarce. Every adult male Jew has to pay an annual half-shekel tax to the temple in coin, but otherwise, families pay their due in figs, olive oil, grain, or fish. Farmers have no

[LEFT] *One side of a half shekel coin from after Jesus's time showing a chalice. It was minted in AD 66 when the Jewish war against Rome was at its height.* [Hoberman Collection/ Corbis]

[RIGHT] *The other side of a half shekel coin showing three pomegranates.* [Hoberman Collection/ Corbis]

way of avoiding the taxes, because they must travel to Sepphoris to sell their harvest. The hated taxman is always on hand when they arrive at their destination. Fishermen have it no better. They are levied special rights fees for permission to drop their nets or dock in a port, and are required to give up a portion of their daily catch.

Because Joseph is a skilled tradesman, he is able to pay his taxes. Indeed, most people in Galilee can do the same—but just barely. Many Galileans suffer malnutrition because they have so little food left for themselves. In the throes of that hunger, they quietly seethe.

Man sowing seeds in ancient times. [Alamy]

The great legends of the Jewish people speak of heroes of their faith rising up to defeat foreign invaders. The people long for the glory days of King David, so many hundreds of years ago, when the

Jews were their own masters and God was the undisputed most powerful force in the cosmos. The residents of Galilee are independent thinkers. They persist in the belief that they will ultimately control their destiny.

In that belief, there is hope. The hardships of working the land and the cruelty of Rome have bred a growing faith in the power of the Jewish God, to whom they pray for rescue and relief. This is the world Jesus of Nazareth inhabits. These are the prayers he hears poured forth every day. The promise of God's deliverance is the one shaft of daylight that comforts the oppressed people of Galilee. Someday, if they can just hold on, God will send someone to make things right, as he did with Abraham, Moses, Daniel, Samson, and David.

How much Jesus is affected by the suffering and anger in his town is unknown. He grows into a strong man, respectful of his parents. Joseph dies sometime between Jesus's thirteenth and thirtieth birthdays, leaving Jesus the family business. He remains devoted to his mother—and she to him. But as he passes his thirtieth birthday, Jesus of Nazareth knows the time has come to fulfill his destiny. Silence is no longer an option. He decides to reveal himself.

It is a decision that will change the world.

It is also a decision that will lead to an agonizing death.

Moses and the tablets with the Ten Commandments and King David with a harp. Painting by Albrecht Dürer for an altarpiece, 1511. [The Bridgeman Art Library]

BOOK II

JESUS
the PREACHER

CHAPTER 7

JOHN BAPTIZES JESUS

AD 26 ✦ JORDAN RIVER ✦ MIDDAY

JOHN THE BAPTIST STANDS WAIST DEEP IN THE COLD, brown Jordan River, waiting patiently as the next pilgrim wades out to stand at his side. He looks to the shore, where many other believers are lined up despite the heat, to be cleansed of their sins.

The believers are mostly poor working people. They have been inspired by John and his radical teachings. The long-haired young man with the sunburned skin and scraggly beard has disciplined himself by living alone in the desert, eating only locusts for protein and honey for energy. He wears a coarse tunic stitched from the skin of a camel and has a simple leather belt tied around his waist. Some think John eccentric, others consider him a rebel, but all agree that he has boldly

Marble statue in the Saint-Roch Church in Paris of the baptism of Jesus, made in the 1700s by Jean-Baptiste Lemoyne. [The Bridgeman Art Library]

Baptism in First-Century Jewish Culture

The word *baptize* comes from an old Greek word, *baptizein*, which means "to dip." Many religious traditions, some old and some new, use water to symbolize purity. In some, water is poured over a person's head. In others, like the Jewish practice of the first century, a person was submerged, or dipped, in water.

Baptism was a common practice in Judea and Galilee. Adults, not infants, were baptized. And they could be baptized as often as they had sins to confess. The Jews believed that when they were cleansed by water, they became pure and would be ready for their savior when he arrived. It was also essential to be pure when they took part in festival rituals. The *mikvah* pools outside Jerusalem in which pilgrims bathed served that purpose before Passover, Pentecost, and the Feast of Tabernacles.

It wasn't necessary that a particular person, such as a rabbi or a priest, perform the baptism. People could quietly name their sins and then wash in water. John the Baptist was thought to be especially close to God, and many people felt he could more effectively take away their sins.

Site on the Jordan River where Jesus is said to have been baptized by John. [Library of Congress]

promised them something that neither Rome nor the temple high priests in Jerusalem can offer: hope.

The end of the known world is coming, John preaches. A new king will arrive to stand in judgment. Wade into the water and be cleansed of your sins, or this newly anointed ruler—this "Christ"—will punish you in the most horrible manner possible. It is a message both religious and political, one that directly challenges the Roman Empire and the hierarchy of the Jewish temple.

John extends an arm as the next pilgrim draws near to stand at his side in the river. He listens intently as the man confesses his many sins. Then John prays for him and says, "After me comes the one more powerful than I, the straps of whose sandals I am not worthy to stoop down and untie. I baptize you with water, but he will baptize you with the Holy Spirit."

John places one hand in the center of the man's back and slowly guides him down into the water, holds him under for a few seconds, and then lifts the man back to his feet. The relieved pilgrim, his sins now forgiven, wades back to shore. Before he has even reached the bank, another believer is walking into the water to be cleansed.

"Who *are* you?" demands a voice from the shore. John has been waiting for this question. Three groups of people are watching him. This question comes from a Pharisee, a temple high priest, sent from Jerusalem to judge whether or not John is committing heresy. The priest is not alone, having made the journey in the company of other Pharisees and Sadducees.

"I am *not* the Christ," John shouts back. The high priests know that he is referring to the person who will fulfill the prophecy—the new Jewish king, a man like Saul, David, and Solomon, the great rulers of generations past who were handpicked by God to lead the Israelites.

"Then who are you?" demands another of the Pharisees. "Are you Elijah?"

John has heard this comparison before. Like him, Elijah was a prophet who preached that the world would soon end.

"No," John replies firmly.

"Who *are* you?" the priests demand once again. "Give us an answer to take back to those who sent us."

John speaks of a prediction made by the prophet Isaiah, a man who lived eight hundred years before. In this particular prediction, Isaiah had foretold that a man would come to tell the people about the day the world would end and God would appear on earth. This man would be "a voice of one calling in the wilderness, 'Prepare the way for the Lord, make straight paths for him.'"

John truly believes that he is the man of whom Isaiah wrote, and he feels obligated to travel from city to city, telling one and all that the end of the world is near and that they must prepare by being baptized.

"Who *are* you?" the priests demand once again, their voices angrier and more insistent.

"I am the voice of one," John responds, "calling in the wilderness."

✦ ✦ ✦ ✦ ✦

The temple priests are not the only officials keeping a close eye on John the Baptist. From his stunning new capital city of Tiberius, shrewdly named after the Roman emperor now in power, Herod Antipas, the tetrarch of Galilee, has sent spies to the Jordan River to track John's every movement. The Baptist is the talk of Galilee, and Antipas fears that this charismatic evangelist will convince the people to rise up against him.

Herod Antipas has spent a great deal of time in Rome, educating himself in Roman ways and customs and absorbing their fondness for literature, poetry, and music. The Jewish Antipas even dresses like Roman aristocracy, wearing the draped piece of cloth known as a toga, rather than the simple robes of the Jewish people.

During his time in Rome, Antipas has learned to douse his food with fermented fish sauce, a pickled condiment with a strong taste that masks spoilage from lack of refrigeration. It is one of many Roman customs he has adopted.

Herod alienated the people of Galilee when he divorced his wife to marry the former wife of his half brother. His new wife, Herodias, knows that the Jews disapprove of her and her marriage. But Herod

A Roman man wore a toga. Woodcut. [North Wind Picture Archives]

Stone excavated from Caesarea that indicates that Pontius Pilate is dedicating a building to Caesar Augustus. [The Bridgeman Art Library]

Antipas, now approaching fifty, understands that his first allegiance is to Emperor Tiberius. Even though Antipas has great power over the Jewish peasants, he must do as Rome tells him to do. He can never comment negatively on anything Tiberius does—even though the Jews are becoming more disenchanted every day with Roman rule. Fear of Tiberius also prevents Antipas from making any reforms that would help the Jewish people. Caught in the middle, he keeps his mouth shut and accumulates as much wealth as he can.

The third person tracking John is the new prefect, or governor, of Judea, the Roman Pontius Pilate. Pilate is a member of the equestrian class and a former soldier from central Italy, appointed to his post by the emperor. His chief function is to keep law and order in his land. He also collects taxes and sits in judgment of people accused of committing crimes.

Pilate is married to Claudia Procula, who has accompanied him to

Judea. It is a dismal appointment, for Judea is known to be a very difficult place to govern. But if her husband excels in this remote diplomatic posting, Claudia hopes that the powers in Rome might make his next assignment somewhere more prestigious.

Pilate knows that his personal and professional future depend on making Tiberius happy. Despite his own pagan beliefs and lifestyle, Tiberius admires the Jews' religious ways. He considers them the most devout subjects in the empire when it comes to keeping the Sabbath holy. Tiberius sends an order to Pontius Pilate instructing him to change nothing already sanctioned by custom, and to regard the Jews themselves, and their laws, as a sacred trust.

According to Tiberius's orders, Pilate is not to meddle in matters of Jewish law. He soon gets his first example of the powers of his subjects' faith.

One of Pilate's first official acts is to order Roman troops in Jerusalem to decorate their banners with busts of Emperor Tiberius. When the people rise up to protest these graven images, which are forbidden by Jewish law, Pilate responds by having his soldiers surround the protesters and draw their swords as if to attack. The Jews refuse to back down. Instead, they bend forward and extend their necks, making it clear that they are prepared to die for their beliefs.

Pilate orders his men to back away. The banners are removed.

Pilate now finds a new strategy for dealing with the Jews, one honoring that "sacred trust." He deliberately develops a strong bond with the high priest Caiaphas, the figurehead of the Jewish faith, the most powerful priest in the Jerusalem temple and the most

influential man in the city. Caiaphas is from a family of priests and lives in a lavish home in the Upper City. He has complete power over religious life in Jerusalem, including the enforcement of Jewish law—even if that means suggesting a sentence that condemns a man or woman to death.

Caiaphas controls the temple treasury, which holds untold riches. He controls the temple police force and all the other people who work there. And Caiaphas is the head of the Sanhedrin, the council of high priests who hear cases concerning religious law. But while Caiaphas and the Sanhedrin may oversee lesser sentences, it is the Roman governor who determines whether or not a death sentence should be carried out.

Pilate is a Roman pagan. Caiaphas is a Jew. They worship differently, eat different foods, have different hopes for their future, and grew up speaking different tongues. Pilate serves at the behest of a divine emperor, while Caiaphas believes he serves at the behest of God. But they share a belief that they are entitled to do anything in order to stay in power.

In this way, state and faith keep a

The Roman god Jupiter, god of the skies and the law. Hand-colored woodcut. [North Wind Picture Archives]

[LEFT] *Photograph of the remains of the house of Caiaphas, the high priest.* [Corbis]

stranglehold on Judea. Caiaphas plays his role in this partnership, sending the team of religious authorities out into the wilderness to cast a critical eye on the ministry of John the Baptist.

✦   ✦   ✦   ✦   ✦

The next day, John stands again in the Jordan River. As usual, the sun shines hot, and long lines of believers wait their turn to be baptized.

In the distance, John sees a man walking down to the river. Like himself, this man has long hair and a beard. He wears sandals and a simple robe. His shoulders are broad, as if he is a workingman. He looks younger than John, but not by much. It is Jesus of Nazareth.

As the crowd of pilgrims looks on, John motions toward Jesus. Jesus wades down into the water and takes his place alongside John, waiting to be baptized. When Jesus rises from being immersed in the water, a dove lands on his shoulder. Jesus makes no move to shoo it away—the bird is quite content to remain there.

John says to the crowd, "Look, the Lamb of God. I saw the Spirit come down from heaven as a dove and remain on him. And I myself did not know him, but the one who sent me to baptize with water told me, 'The man on whom you see the Spirit come down and remain is he who will baptize with the Holy Spirit.' I have seen and I testify that this is God's Chosen One."

The believers drop to their knees and press their faces to the earth.

John is dumbstruck. "I need to be baptized by *you*, and yet you come to me?"

Temple Hierarchy

Caiaphas, a member of the Sadducee sect, was the high priest at the time of Jesus. His father-in-law, Annas, had been high priest before him. Caiaphas controlled the massive temple treasury and all of the thousands of people who worked in the temple—the priests, the guards, the choirs and musicians, the teachers, and the many workers.

The Sadducees were aristocratic priests, many from families of priests. They were less rigid in interpreting the law and more willing to live in harmony with the pagan Romans. The Sadducees were very involved with the rituals at the temple. They cared about appearance and were literal followers of the customs set down in the Torah.

Pharisees were common people and were respected because they specialized in interpreting the oral laws God gave to Moses. The Mosaic Law and the Torah, the written Scripture, formed the basis of Jewish religious and legal custom. It was the Pharisees who interpreted Mosaic Law and wrote their ideas down in the Talmud. The Pharisees believed that a Messiah would come and bring with him an era of world peace. Nicodemus was a Pharisee.

Members of both the Pharisees and the Sadducees made up the Sanhedrin, the seventy-one-member high court that was responsible for running the temple, collecting taxes, and interpreting religious and civil laws. But the Sanhedrin, of course, was not independent. Rome was always watching its actions and decisions.

A high priest at the temple dressed for the Feast of Tabernacles. [Mary Evans Picture Library]

Jesus does not clarify his identity to the crowd. But speaking softly with John the Baptist, Jesus does declare who he is. Bowing his head to accept the water, he tells John, "Let it be so now; it is proper for us to do this to fulfill all righteousness."

John places one hand on Jesus's back and slowly lowers him into the water. "I baptize you with water for repentance," John says as he submerges Jesus in the current.

He then lifts Jesus to his feet.

"This is the Son of God," John cries out.

"Son of God" is a regal title indicative of the Messiah, a title attributed to King David. It is believed that when the Messiah returns, he will be king of the Jews, in keeping with David, the perfect king. The people now looking on understand "the Son of God" to mean the anointed one who is coming as ruler and king.

The crowd remains on its knees as Jesus steps onto the shore and keeps on walking. He is headed alone into the desert to fast for forty days and nights. It is a journey he makes willingly, knowing that he must confront and defeat any and all temptation in order to make his mind and body pure before publicly preaching his message of faith and hope.

John the Baptist's work is now done. But his fate has been sealed.

John is that rarest of all prophets—a man who lives to see his predictions come true. The people still desire to be cleansed of their sins through baptism, and huge crowds continue to trail John wherever he goes. If anything, his following is growing even larger. And while there is no longer a need to prophesy the coming of a new Christ, John has a powerful gift for speaking. He is not the sort to remain silent about immorality and injustice. So when John learns that Herod Antipas has divorced his wife and then violated Jewish law by taking his half brother's former spouse for his new bride, he cannot remain silent. Walking the countryside, John the Baptist loudly denounces Antipas wherever he goes, turning the people against their ruler.

Antipas orders the spies who have been keeping an eye on John to arrest him. John is chained, then marched fifteen miles through the hot desert. Finally, he sees a vision in front of him. It is Antipas's mountaintop fortress at Machaerus.

Ruins of Machaerus, fortress of Herod the Great and, later, Antipas. [Corbis]

John is then forced to walk three thousand feet up to the citadel, which is surrounded on all sides by rocky ravines.

The view from the palace, which lies in the center of the fortified structure, is stunning. If John were allowed to enjoy it, he might be able to see the slender brown curves of his beloved Jordan River snaking through the valley so far below. And perhaps John does pause for a final glimpse as he is marched through the great wooden doors that allow entrance to the citadel. But those doors close behind him all too quickly. Still in chains, he is marched into Antipas's throne room, where he stands defiant and fearless before this man. And even when given a chance to recant his charges, John does not. "It is not lawful," he tells the ruler, "for you to have your brother's wife."

The woman in question, Herodias, sits at Antipas's side. John is not only condemning her husband, but herself as well, but she sees that Antipas is actually fearful of John, and is afraid to order his death. Herodias, however, is a patient woman and knows that she will find a way to exact her revenge. How dare this unkempt savage insult her?

And so it is that John is hurled into the dungeons of Machaerus, there to rot until Antipas sets him free—or Herodias has him killed.

Meanwhile, a far greater threat to Antipas is beginning to emerge. Jesus of Nazareth has now embarked on a spiritual journey—a mission that will challenge the world's most powerful men.

CHAPTER 8

TURNING OUT THE MONEYLENDERS

APRIL, AD 27 ✦ JERUSALEM ✦ DAY

SINCE HIS BAPTISM AND TIME SPENT FASTING IN THE desert, Jesus's ministry has been a quiet one. Today that will change.

Jesus makes his way up the steps to the temple courts. Passover pilgrims surround him. Hundreds of thousands of Jewish believers have once again traveled a great distance—from Galilee, Syria, Egypt, and even Rome—to celebrate the climax to the Jewish year. Not that they have a choice: According to Jewish law, failure to visit the temple during Passover is one of thirty-six violations of Mosaic Law that will result in the holy punishment of *karet*—being spiritually cut off from God. Those who disobey will suffer a premature death or other punishment known only to the deity. So as he has done every spring since childhood, Jesus of Nazareth makes the trek to Jerusalem.

The spiritual emotion that flows through the city is wondrous, as these many Jews come together to openly celebrate their faith and sing praises to God. Agents of the temple have repaired the dirt roads coming into town to make them smooth after the hard winter rains. Special pools, called *mikvot*, are dug so that the travelers can immerse themselves in the ritual bath, in order to be pure upon entering the holy city.

After immersing himself in the *mikvah*, Jesus enters Jerusalem. Inside the city walls, he sees the hundreds of temporary clay ovens that have been constructed in order that each pilgrim will have a place to roast his Passover sacrifice before sitting down to the evening Seder feast. He hears the bleat of sheep as shepherds and their flocks clog the narrow streets. And Jesus can well imagine the peal of the silver trumpets and harmonious voices of the choir that will echo in the courts of the inner temple, just moments before a lamb is slaughtered for the Passover sacrifice. A priest will catch its blood in a gold bowl and then sprinkle it on the altar as the lamb is hung on a hook and skinned. The prayers of thanksgiving will soon follow, and the temple courts will echo with songs of hallelujah. The meat will be given to the family to cook for their Seder meal in one of the many communal ovens set up in the city. The skin of the animal was given to the priests.

This is Passover in Jerusalem. It has been this way since the rebuilding of the temple. Each Passover is unique in its glory and personal stories, but the rituals remain the same.

Now, as he steps into the Court of the Gentiles, Jesus prepares to make this Passover different.

✦　✦　✦　✦　✦

In the partially enclosed temple courts, tables piled with coins line one wall, shaded by the temple awnings. They are lorded over by scheming men known as *shulhani*—money changers. Long lines of out-of-towners await their chance to exchange their Roman coins into shekels, the only currency accepted in the temple. The Roman coins have images of gods or portraits of the emperor on them, and it is against Jewish law to use them in the temple. Shekels are decorated with images of plants and other nonhuman objects. Pilgrims must use shekels to pay the annual tax and to purchase animals for ritual slaughter.

Ritual Sacrifice

In the ancient world, many cultures sacrificed animals to their god or gods, believing that the blood of the creature would please. In Jesus's world, the Romans and Greeks as well as the Jews practiced animal sacrifice.

Ritual sacrifice was required by the Law of Moses. It could take place only at the temple in Jerusalem. This was not a custom that was part of life in synagogues in towns or cities, or in private homes.

At the temple, priests alone could perform ritual sacrifices. A pilgrim purchased an animal, an unblemished male lamb, for example, from a vendor in the courtyards surrounding the temple. He gave a priest the lamb, which was slaughtered. Its blood was sprinkled around the altar. The priest then returned some of the lamb to the pilgrim, and it was the central part of that family's feast meal. The priest kept the skin of the animal. It was salted and stored in a room adjacent to the temple.

Pilgrims and residents of Jerusalem offered animals for sacrifice as a way of

A typical man in Jerusalem as drawn by James Tissot in the 19th century.
[Mary Evans Picture Library]

giving a gift to God. Other gifts offered were firstfruits, or the first results of a harvest, and money, called a tithe. Gifts were offered for several reasons—to honor God, in thanksgiving for a good event, such as the birth of a child or a good harvest, or in supplication, asking for forgiveness or favor. The custom of ritual sacrifice came to an end after the Romans destroyed the temple in Jerusalem in AD 70.

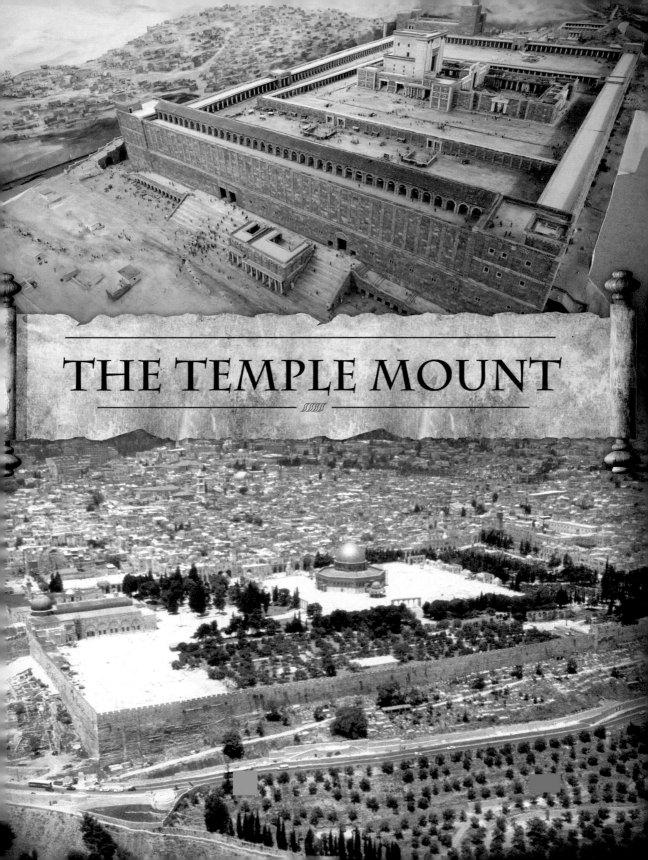

THE TEMPLE MOUNT

THEN AND NOW

T HE TEMPLE IN ANCIENT Jerusalem was the center of Jewish life. The site of the Temple Complex—called Mount Moriah—had long been considered sacred by the Jewish people. It was believed to be the place where God gathered dust to make Adam and where Abraham brought his son Isaac to be sacrificed.

In 957 BC, the first building on the site was completed under the direction of King Solomon. Also called the First Temple, Solomon's Temple, and its surrounding courtyards, was a place of worship as well as a place to teach and learn. Most important, it was the resting place of the Ark of the Covenant—the sacred vessel that stored the stone tablets on which the Ten Commandments were written. Those tablets disappeared when the First Temple was destroyed by invading Babylonians in 586 BC.

Seventy years later on the same site, construction began on a new sanctuary, which was finished in 516 BC. In the first century BC, King Herod expanded the structure and its grounds, developing an area of 36 acres. More than 10,000 laborers worked for 23 years—literally moving the mountain—to complete the renovation. The resulting Temple Mount complex—called Herod's Temple or the Second Temple—is the place where Jesus visited and taught. However, scholars do not know precisely what it looked like; all that remains in present-day Jerusalem is the Western Wall.

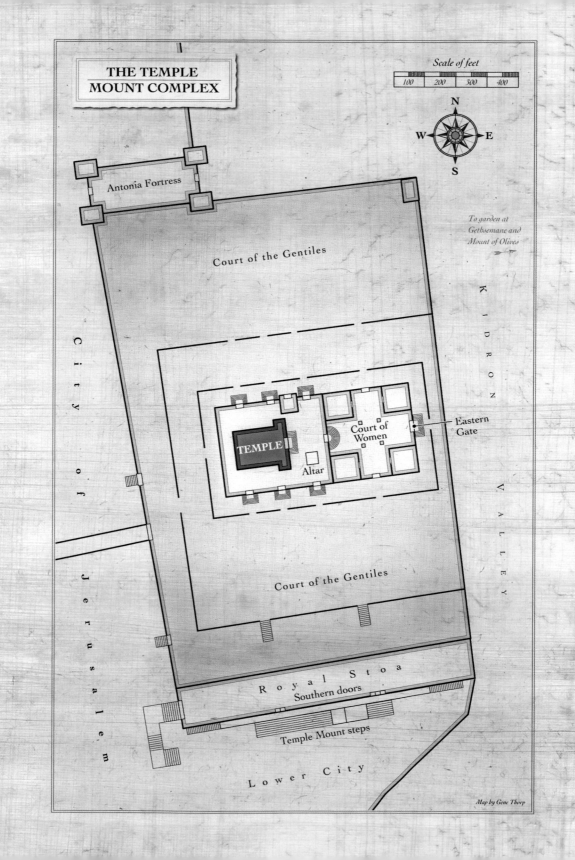

BRINGING THE TEMPLE TO LIFE

The model, photographed here by Geoff Robinson, is a 1:100 scale replica of the Temple Mount built by English farmer and lay preacher Alec Garrard. Using archaeological research as well as biblical passages and scholarly articles, the late Mr. Garrard constructed the 12-by-20-foot model with painstaking precision. He also sculpted 4,000 half-inch tall clay figures—baking, painting, and posing each one individually.

The Temple Mount complex was designed as a series of courtyards decreasing in size and increasing in importance, culminating in the Temple itself. Since thousands, and sometimes millions, of visitors approached the Temple Mount, the area surrounding the Temple on two sides was vibrant with shops and markets. Traders from around the Roman Empire set up stalls to sell and barter goods. The eastern side of the platform fell away sharply into the Kidron Valley. The Antonia Fortress, a military structure for soldiers, occupied the northern side.

The Second Temple viewed from the southeast. Expansive
steps lead to the southern doors of the Temple Mount.

Up the grand steps and through the southern doors was the Royal Stoa, a vast covered porch. One hundred sixty-two pillars supported this portico and its second level. A visitor could find relief from the heat and rain in its shelter. And it is here that the money-changers and lenders had their tables. The Sanhedrin met in a room at one end of this grand hallway.

Between the covered porches and the next ring of walls was the Court of the Gentiles, so named because it was the only place inside that non-Jews could visit; to go any farther toward the Temple itself, however, one had to be Jewish.

Traders—mostly controlled by Annas, Caiaphas's father—sold animals for sacrifice, food and drink for visitors, and other goods. People also made fires to roast the meat of the animals they offered for sacrifice.

The Gate of the Pure and Just was on the northeastern side of the Court of the Gentiles. Only Jewish people could pass beyond this to the inner areas of the Temple. Directly inside the gates was the Court of Women, also called the Court of Prayer. This was as far as women could venture into the complex.

Standing high above the Court of Women were four enormous golden oil lamps with five branches. Women worshipped on the balconies surrounding three sides of this court. Men worshipped below. Senior rabbis taught under the portico.

On the Feast of Tabernacles, men climbed from the second story above the Court of Women to light the lamps.

◆ ——————————————— ◆

The gate leading from the Court of Women farther into the complex was surrounded by a graceful staircase from which rabbis sometimes preached. People left their offerings and sacrifices at the top of the steps for priests. The altar of burnt sacrifice and the Temple doors, decorated with golden vines, can be seen in the background.

Only priests and rabbis could enter the Temple. In the courtyard outside the Temple doors stood the altar of the burnt offering and the laver, a huge cauldron of water. Animals to be sacrificed were held in pens here. Their blood was sprinkled around the altar. The laver, which was used by the priests to wash, was drained and refilled each day.

The Temple itself was visited by only the most senior high priests. Inside were places for ritual worship, including an altar of incense, a table to display bread before God, and a golden seven-branched lamp.

At the northwest corner of the Temple Mount was the Antonia Fortress, the headquarters and barracks for Roman soldiers in Jerusalem. It was initially built on this mountain to provide a high vantage point from which to guard the city. The fortress courtyard was large enough for many ranks of legionnaires to assemble.

Temple courtyards were bustling places. Of course, pilgrims came on holy days to pray during liturgy, to study the Torah with one of the many teachers there, to ask questions of the scholars, and to make offerings to God. But the complex was also a gathering place, a meeting place, and a public square where people chatted, met friends, and found relief from the heat of the city.

TEMPLE MOUNT TODAY

◆ ——————————— ◆

Herod's Temple was destroyed in AD 70 when the Romans over-ran Jerusalem, successfully stamping out a Jewish revolt. Early Christians built shrines and churches in Jerusalem. In AD 638, Muslims captured the Temple site. They built the magnificent Dome of the Rock from ca. AD 687 to AD 691. The oldest Islamic monument in the world, the Dome covers the rock from which Muhammad is said to have ascended into heaven.

The money changers demand unfair exchange rates for the privilege of turning Roman money into shekels. The temple high priests also profit from this arrangement. Within the temple's inner courts are massive vaults filled with shekels and foreign coins exchanged each year by pilgrims. When that money is lent by the temple—as it so often is to peasants who need help paying their taxes—the interest rates are extremely high. All debts are tallied on ledger sheets kept within the inner temple's grand vaults, and those who can-

A Roman coin bearing the likeness of Augustus Caesar found in Jerusalem. [Corbis]

not repay suffer severe indignities: the loss of a home, loss of land and livestock, and eventually, life as a debt slave or membership in the "unclean" class. The slums of lower Jerusalem are packed with families who were driven from their land because they could not repay money they borrowed from the temple.

So while Passover might be a time of faith and piety, it is also about money. As many as four million Jews make their way to Jerusalem each year, adding to the sixty thousand people who usually live there. This means much more income for local shop owners and innkeepers, but the temple priests and their Roman masters get most of the profit through taxation and money changing. Even more money is made when the poor must buy a lamb or dove for the mandatory Passover sacrifice. If a priest inspects the animal or bird

and finds even a single blemish, the sacrifice will be deemed unclean, and the peasant will be forced to buy another. It is no wonder that the people quietly seethe when doing business with the temple priests.

Today Jesus climbs to the Court of Gentiles and makes his way into the broad open-air plaza. Since his baptism and time spent fasting in the desert, his ministry has been a quiet one.

But now, Jesus walks past the tables piled high with coins and sees the people of Galilee standing so helplessly before these greedy money changers and the haughty high priests. This Passover ritual of money changing has not altered since he was a child, but on this day, Jesus feels he must do something about this obvious wrong.

Jesus is not normally prone to anger or fits of rage. In fact, he usually exudes a powerful serenity. So when he boldly storms toward the money changers' tables, those who know him become alarmed. There is a power to Jesus's gait and a steely determination to his gaze.

The tables are made of wood. Their surfaces are scarred and dented from the thousands of coins that have been pushed back and forth across the tabletops. The money changers sit before enormous piles of currency, gleaming in the strong Jerusalem sun.

Heavy as they might be, the weight of the tables does not bother Jesus—not after twenty years of hauling lumber and stone alongside his father. He places his hands beneath the nearest table and flips it over. A small fortune in coins flies in every direction. And even as the stunned *shulhani* cry out in a rage and coins cascade down onto the stone courtyard, Jesus is already at the next table and then on to the next.

Nobody has ever seen anything like this. This behavior is an act of madness, the sort of thing that could get a man killed. As the crowd gasps in shock, Jesus flashes a whip he has made from cords of rope. He moves from the money changers' tables to where goats and sheep are being sold. He cracks the whip, sending the animals running. Jesus marches over to the cages of doves that are also being sold for slaughter and opens the doors to set them free.

And nobody tries to stop him.

"Get these out of here!" he shouts to the men selling doves. "Stop turning my Father's house into a market!"

These men, who enjoyed absolute power over the pilgrims just moments ago, now cower, terrified that Jesus will turn his whip on them. The money changers see their fortunes littering the ground but make no move to pick up the coins. Livestock run loose across the Court of the Gentiles—cows, goats, and sheep galloping aimlessly through the throngs, their rendezvous with the slaughtering knife temporarily on hold.

Suddenly, a circle of pilgrims and temple officials forms around Jesus, who holds his whip firmly in one hand, as if daring them to challenge him. "What sign can you show us to prove your authority to do all this?" demands a money changer. Despite the commotion, soldiers do not run in to quell the disturbance. Better to let this madman explain himself.

"Destroy this temple," Jesus vows, "and I will raise it again in three days."

Now they know he's insane. "It has taken forty-six years to build this temple, and you are going to raise it in three days?" scoffs a money changer. Among the onlookers is Nicodemus, a devout Pharisee and a member of the Jewish ruling council, who watches with interest and waits for the answer to the question.

But Jesus says nothing. He knows his words will not change the hearts and minds of the temple leaders. Although one watches him with more curiosity than anger.

No one blocks Jesus's path as he leaves the Court of the Gentiles and walks toward the temple itself. Behind him is the clink of silver and bronze as the money changers scurry to sweep up every last coin. The men selling livestock race to gather up their beasts. It is the pilgrims who continue to marvel at what they have just witnessed. Many of them have dreamed of committing such a bold act. From his Galilean accent and simple robes to his workingman's physique, it is clear that Jesus is one of them. For some, this man is a hero. And his actions will be discussed everywhere.

CHAPTER 9

NICODEMUS QUESTIONS JESUS

APRIL, AD 27 ✦ JERUSALEM

NIGHT IN JERUSALEM IS A TIME OF QUIET CELEBRATION, as pilgrims pack into local courtyards and inns to bed down. It is customary to open one's home for the visitors, and to do so with a glad heart. There is not enough room to house all the travelers in the city, so many camp on the steep hillsides and valleys outside the city walls. From the thick groves of trees on the Mount of Olives, across the Kidron Valley, and down toward the Old City of David, which lies just south of the temple, families and friends spread out their blankets and bedrolls to spend the night under the stars.

Among them is Jesus. He has returned to the temple time and again during his Passover stay, teaching from that temple cloister known as Solomon's Porch. This is his favorite place in the temple, and even when he is not listening to the scholars or joining in to offer his own teachings about the kingdom of

God, Jesus often lingers in that area. Wherever he goes, crowds now flock to him, asking questions about God's kingdom and listening reverently to his answers. Jesus is comfortable in public. He enjoys people and speaks eloquently, often using stories to illuminate his teachings.

Jesus has made a deep impression in a short amount of time. His dramatic assault against the money changers seems to have paid off.

Photograph of the Mount of Olives taken between 1860 and 1880. [Library of Congress LOT 7741]

He has made an impression on another group as well—the Pharisees, the temple leaders who obsess about all aspects of Jewish law, are paying particular attention. They are skeptical about Jesus and would like specific information before passing religious judgment on him.

Now, under cover of darkness, the Pharisee Nicodemus, who enjoys a powerful role as a member of the Jewish ruling council, approaches Jesus. He has chosen nighttime because it would be awkward for him to say what is on his mind in the midday temple courts, where even the lowliest peasant could hear his words. And Nicodemus also knows that this quiet hour means that he can have an uninterrupted discussion with Jesus.

"Rabbi," Nicodemus begins

Oak statue of Nicodemus carved in France in the 1600s. [The Bridgeman Art Library] deferentially, stepping into the light cast by the flames. If Jesus is surprised to see such an exalted Pharisee stepping from the darkness, he does not let on. "We know that you are a teacher who has come from God," Nicodemus continues, speaking for his fellow Pharisees.

"Very truly I tell you, no one can see the kingdom of God unless they are born again," Jesus replies. He has been telling all who listen that a person must be spiritually reborn to be judged kindly by God.

This is a new concept to the Pharisees. Nicodemus asks in astonishment, "How can someone be born when they are old? Surely they cannot enter a second time into their mother's womb to be born!"

"Flesh gives birth to flesh," Jesus replies, "but the Spirit gives birth to spirit. You should not be surprised at my saying, 'You must be born again.'"

Nicodemus is thoroughly confused. "How can this be?" he asks.

"You are Israel's teacher, and do you not understand these things?" Jesus asks. If he is uncomfortable scolding one of the most powerful religious leaders in Jerusalem, it does not show. "For God so loved the world that he gave his one and only Son, that whoever believes in him shall not perish but have eternal life. For God did not send his Son into the world to condemn the world, but to save the world through him."

Nicodemus is intrigued but frustrated. He is a man dedicated to stated religious law. Now Jesus is telling him that God is about love, not rules. And that the Son of God has come to save the world, even insinuating that this is *his* true identity. Then he adds words about being reborn, as if such a thing were humanly possible.

Nicodemus has heard Jesus teaching in the temple courts, so he knows that he likes to speak in parables, stories that illustrate a religious or moral principle. Though Nicodemus may not fully understand them, Jesus's statements have given him a great deal to think about as he walks alone back up the hill into Jerusalem.

✦   ✦   ✦   ✦   ✦

Jesus has spent the months since returning from Jerusalem traveling through Galilee, teaching in synagogues. He has become popular, praised everywhere he goes for the depth and insights of his teaching. There is mystery about him, too. No one can explain how this man with no medical knowledge healed a dying child in the fishing village of Capernaum. And stories are circulating about unexpected bounty suddenly appearing at a wedding in Cana he went to with his mother. Now Jesus is back home in Nazareth sitting among the townspeople he has known all his life.

The men of Nazareth pray, their voices blending together as one: "Hear, O Israel: the Lord our God, the Lord is One. Love the Lord your God with all your heart and with all your soul and with all your strength."

It is the Sabbath day, and the Shema marks the beginning of the Sabbath worship. The synagogue is a small square room with

Sea of Galilee at Capernaum; about 1900. [Library of Congress LC-M32-A-224]

wooden benches against each wall. The temple in Jerusalem, with its priests and vaults and animal sacrifices, is the center of Jewish life. The local synagogue, however, is an intimate place where believers worship and teach, taking turns reading from the parchment scrolls on which the Scriptures are written. In the synagogue, there are no high priests, clergy, or standard liturgy, and anyone is allowed to play the part of rabbi, or teacher. Also, there is no money on the tables.

Jesus joins in as the men of Nazareth lift their voices in song, chanting the words of the Psalms.

Then an attendant hands Jesus the scroll with the words of the prophet Isaiah. "The Spirit of the Lord is on me," Jesus reads in Hebrew, "because he has anointed me to proclaim good news to the poor. He has sent me to proclaim freedom for the prisoners and recovery of sight for the blind, to set the oppressed free, to proclaim the year of the Lord's favor."

Jesus remains standing, translating the words he has just read into Aramaic for the benefit of those not fluent in Hebrew. It is customary to stand while reading, then sit while teaching. So now he sits and presses his back against the wall, aware that all eyes are upon him. "Today this scripture is fulfilled in your hearing," Jesus calmly informs them.

The crowd is shocked.

"Isn't this Joseph's son?" they ask. For while they know the answer, the words are a reminder that Jesus should remember his place: his family is not the wealthiest in town, nor is he the smartest among them. He is the son of Joseph and nothing more. In their eyes, Jesus exalting himself as the man sent by God to preach the good news is offensive.

But Jesus doesn't back down. He has been expecting this response. "Truly I tell you," he predicts, "no prophet is accepted in his hometown." Disregarding that they are in a house of worship, some men leap to their feet and prepare to attack. Moving quickly, Jesus races out the door. But they follow. Working together, the men who had been praying just moments ago now cut off any route of escape. Jesus is forced to the edge of town, where a tall cliff provides a commanding view of Galilee.

The men's intention is to hurl Jesus to his death. And it appears that might happen, for Jesus seems powerless. But at the last minute, he turns to face his detractors. Drawing himself up to his full height, Jesus squares his shoulders and holds his ground. He is not a menacing man, but he has a commanding presence and displays an utter lack of fear. The words he says next will never be written down, nor will the insults these men continue to hurl at him ever be chronicled. In the end, the mob parts and Jesus walks away unscathed.

And he keeps walking.

✦ ✦ ✦ ✦ ✦

Jesus has issued three pronouncements about his identity—one to the public in Jerusalem, one to Nicodemus the Pharisee, and the third in the intimate setting of his own town synagogue, to the people he knows best of all. Three times he has declared himself to be the Son of God, a blasphemous statement that could get him killed.

Now Jesus is completely alone, cut off from the life he once knew, destined to wander through Galilee preaching words of hope and love.

Over thousands of years, those words will rally billions of human beings to believe in his preaching. But they will not convert the powerful men who currently hold the life of Jesus in their hands.

To them, Jesus of Nazareth is a marked man.

CHAPTER 10

PREACHING FROM A FISHING BOAT

SUMMER, AD 27 ✦ CAPERNAUM, GALILEE ✦ AFTERNOON

T HE LOCAL FISHING FLEET HAS JUST RETURNED FROM a long night and day on the Sea of Galilee, and great crowds fill the markets along Capernaum's waterfront promenade. A walkway in the center of the market is a focus of activity. Fishermen sort their catches before making the official count for the taxman. Matthew, the taxman, keeps a keen eye on who brings in how many fish, and customers everywhere are eager to purchase the

freshest catch for their evening meal. What doesn't get sold this day will be shipped to Magdala for drying and salting and then will be packed tightly into baskets and exported throughout the Roman Empire. Capernaum is the busiest of all the ports on the Sea of Galilee. So busy that a detachment of one hundred Roman soldiers has been posted here, to ensure that all taxes are collected according to the law—and that those taxes get sent right away to Herod Antipas.

So Jesus has come to the right place if he is looking for an audience—which indeed he is. The problem, however, is that Capernaum is too busy. No one will be able to hear him over the clink of sinker leads dropping onto stone and the haggling between shopkeepers and customers. The fishermen themselves are exhausted from hours of throwing out their fishing nets and hauling them hand over hand back into their boats, and they are in no mood to listen to a sermon.

Jesus stops to look up and down the long, fingerlike row of piers, carefully studying the various fishing boats. He narrows his search to two empty boats. He has met their owners before and now sees them washing and stretching their twenty-foot-wide nets in preparation for the next trip. The two men take care to eliminate knots and tangles, while also replacing any sinker weights that have fallen off. Though he knows next to nothing about fishing, Jesus walks down the pier with confidence and steps into one of the empty craft. No one stops him.

Fishermen with nets in ancient Palestine. Colored engraving, no date. [Alamy]

As he gazes back toward the shoreline, Jesus can see the raised central roof of the town synagogue a block from the water. It stands taller than the homes and waterfront administrative offices, reminding him that Capernaum's citizens worship God and hold a teacher like himself in great reverence.

A fisherman in his early twenties walks to the boat. Simon, as he is known, is a simple, uneducated, and impulsive man. He knows Jesus from a previous meeting during the summer. At the time, Jesus had called upon Simon and his brother Andrew to join him as he walked through Galilee preaching his message. He said they could save souls by becoming "fishers of men." And while Simon initially accepted that call, he also has a wife and mother-in-law to care for. The task of being one of Jesus's disciples and spreading the word is difficult to balance with his need to make a living. His commitment to Jesus has flagged.

But now Jesus is back, standing before him in his boat.

Simon doesn't tell him to leave. He just asks Jesus what he wants. Jesus tells Simon to push the boat away from the dock and drop anchor a little way offshore. The spoken word will carry easily across the lake's surface, and Jesus knows he will be heard by one and all if he teaches from a place on the water.

Simon is exhausted and dejected. He has been up for twenty-four hours, sailing his small boat out onto the lake and dropping his nets again and again and again. His back aches from leaning over the side to pull those nets back in. Simon needs water and a meal. He needs a soft bed. But most of all, he needs to pay his taxes, and last night did nothing to help, for Simon did not catch a single fish.

Perhaps Simon has nothing to do, or perhaps he can't face the thought of returning home to his mother-in-law and wife empty-handed. Perhaps he hopes the teacher will say a few words that will lighten his burden. Or maybe he just feels guilty for going back on his original commitment to Jesus. Whatever the reason, Simon undoes the knot connecting his boat to its anchorage and pushes away from the pier.

Jesus has been standing this whole while. But when Simon's

Sardines. [The Bridgeman Art Library]

boat floats just far enough from the shore that Jesus can be clearly heard, he takes a seat, adopting the traditional pose for teaching.

Thanks to Simon and his boat, Jesus is soon regaling the entire waterfront at Capernaum with his insightful words. As always, people are overcome by his charisma. One by one, they stop what they are doing to listen.

"Put out into deep water," Jesus tells the weary fisherman when he is finished speaking, "and let down the nets for a catch."

"Master," Simon responds, "we've worked hard all night and haven't caught anything."

Sending his boat out into the deep water is the last thing Simon wants to do, yet he also feels powerless to say no.

So with Jesus sitting calmly, Simon hoists the small sail and aims his boat out into the deepest waters of the Sea of Galilee.

A short time later, Jesus and Simon are catching so many fish that the sturdy linen nets start to break. The sheer volume of carp, sardines, and musht threatens to capsize his small craft, and Simon is forced to signal to James and John, the partners in his fishing cooperative, to come help.

Rather than rejoice, Simon is terrified. Ever since the moment Jesus first stepped into his boat, something deeply spiritual about his presence has made Simon uncomfortable. He feels unholy in comparison. Simon throws himself onto his knees on top of the pile of writhing fish and begs Jesus to leave him alone. "Go away from me, Lord; I am a sinful man!"

"Don't be afraid," Jesus tells Simon, "from now on you will fish for people."

And so it is that Simon—whom Jesus renames Peter, meaning "rock"—becomes Jesus's first disciple, or follower. Peter cannot explain why Jesus has selected him for this honor. Why didn't Jesus pick the local rabbi, or the most pious teachers in Capernaum, or even some of the more devout fishermen? Other disciples soon join Jesus, including Matthew, Capernaum's despised local taxman.

By early in the year 28, Jesus has selected twelve men to follow him and learn his teachings, so that they may one day go out alone into the world and preach his message.

Four—Peter, Andrew, James, and John—are fishermen. Jesus has specifically singled out men from this calling because their job requires them to be able to speak and understand many of the local languages—Aramaic, Hebrew, Greek, and even a little Latin. This will allow them to spread the word to a wide group of potential followers.

All the disciples are from Galilee, except one. He is from a town called Carioth—or "Iscariot," as it will one day be translated into the Greek of the Gospels. His name is Judas. He speaks with the polished accent of Judea's southern region and is so good with money that Jesus selects him as the group's treasurer instead of Matthew. Jesus chooses him as one of his twelve disciples and refers to him openly as a friend. One day that will change.

[ABOVE] *Carp.* [Mary Evans Picture Library]

[RIGHT] *Musht, also called St. Peter's fish.* [The Bridgeman Art Library]

CHAPTER 11

THE SERMON ON THE MOUNT

SPRING/SUMMER, AD 27 ✦ OUTSIDE CAPERNAUM

GALILEE IS A SMALL REGION, MEASURING JUST THIRTY by forty miles. Its cities are connected by a series of ancient highways and Roman roads plied daily by traders, pilgrims, and travelers. Jesus chooses Capernaum as his headquarters—and it is a smart choice. The fishing community is constantly sending out its product to far-flung markets, and those who hear Jesus speak in and around that city spread the news about his ministry when they travel from place to place selling their baskets loaded with salted fish.

On some days, Jesus ventures out from Capernaum to preach. The crowds that find him increase as the months pass, and his popularity grows. He teaches in synagogues and in open fields, in private homes and along the lakeshore. Men and women abandon their labors to hear him speak, and vast audiences

The Mount of Beatitudes in Capernaum, thought to be the site of the Sermon on the Mount. [Mary Evans Picture Library]

crowd close together to hear his simple message of God's love and hope.

Not everyone adores him, however. It would seem that a lone man preaching such a noncombative message would not present a problem for Rome. But word has reached the Roman governor, Pilate, about his potential Jewish rebel. The spies of Herod Antipas are also keeping a close eye on Jesus, whom they perceive to be a successor to John the Baptist.

And the Jewish religious authorities in Jerusalem and Galilee,

Today the Church of the Beatitudes sits on the hill above the Sea of Galilee. [Richard T. Nowitz/Corbis]

particularly the Pharisees who make sure people obey religious law, are now watching Jesus closely for any violation. When news of supernatural healings performed by Jesus begins to make the rounds in Galilee, the religious authorities become even more alarmed.

But Jesus does not back down.

Instead, he becomes even more assertive. For the poor and oppressed people of Galilee, the sermon he will soon preach from a mountainside outside Capernaum will define their struggle in a way that will never be forgotten.

"Blessed are the poor in spirit, for theirs is the kingdom of heaven," Jesus begins.

"Blessed are they who mourn, for they will be comforted.

"Blessed are the meek, for they will inherit the earth.

"Blessed are those who hunger and thirst for righteousness, for they will be filled.

"Blessed are the merciful, for they will be shown mercy.

"Blessed are the pure in heart, for they will see God.

"Blessed are the peacemakers, for they will be called children of God.

"Blessed are those who are persecuted because of righteousness, for theirs is the kingdom of heaven."

Jesus is sitting, letting his powerful speaking voice carry his words out to the massive crowd. There are Pharisees among the people. And they are no doubt stunned as Jesus sets forth his own interpretation of religious law. The sermon is intended to remind

The Lord's Prayer in Aramaic and Hebrew in the contemporary Pater Noster Chapel in Jerusalem. [Alamy]

the men and women of Galilee, who feel oppressed and hopeless, that their current circumstances will not last forever.

"This, then, is how you should pray," Jesus tells them. No one speaks. The crowd leans forward, straining to listen.

"Our Father in heaven, hallowed be your name. Your kingdom come, your will be done, on earth as it is in heaven. Give us today our daily bread, and forgive us our debts, as we also have forgiven our debtors. And lead us not into temptation, but deliver us from the evil one."

The crowd is stunned as Jesus finishes. For the peasants of Galilee, his words offer solace for their life under Roman rule: the need to rely on God, the worry about daily nourishment, the constant struggle to stay out of debt, and finally a reminder that in the midst of this cruel life, succumbing to the temptation to lie, cheat, or steal will only lead the people farther and farther away from God.

The powerful words will become known as the Sermon on the Mount and the Lord's Prayer.

The crowds follow Jesus down the mountain that day, through the tall spring grass and small limestone boulders, past the fields of new wheat, trailing him all the way back to Capernaum.

There, soon after entering the city, a most amazing thing happens: the Roman military officer in charge of Capernaum declares himself to be a follower of Jesus.

Jesus is astonished. This admission could end the soldier's career, or even get him killed. Jesus turns to him. "Truly I tell you," he says with emotion, "I have not found anyone in Israel with such great faith."

Legionnaires in regulation armor. Relief. [The Bridgeman Art Library]

CHAPTER 12

MARY OF MAGDALA

FALL, AD 27 ✦ CAPERNAUM

THREE MONTHS AFTER THE SERMON ON THE MOUNT, Jesus is in the home of a Pharisee. He has been invited to dinner to discuss his teachings. The Pharisee, Simon, does not like Jesus. And he is demonstrating his contempt by not playing the role of a good host. Though Jesus walked the four dusty miles from Capernaum to Magdala in sandals to be here, Simon has not provided him with water to wash the dust from his feet, as is the custom. Simon hasn't offered Jesus a respectful kiss of greeting on the cheek, nor rubbed his forehead with olive oil, a common practice of respect to a guest.

There are some six thousand Pharisees in Judea, and their name means "separated ones"—this refers to the way they hold themselves apart from other Jews. The Pharisees, who have appointed themselves guardians of Jewish religious law, believe that their interpretations of Scripture are the only right ones.

But now Jesus has chosen to interpret the Scriptures himself. And the Pharisees are threatened as they watch the people of Galilee eagerly listen to his ideas. So Simon the Pharisee has invited Jesus to dinner with friends to see if they can trap him into saying something blasphemous.

A young woman enters the room silently. She is a prostitute who has heard Jesus speak and who has been invited by Simon to appear this night as part of his elaborate plan to test Jesus. The moment is obviously awkward, for rarely does a sinful woman enter the home of a holy Pharisee. Nevertheless, Mary of Magdala—or Mary Magdalene, as she will go down in history—now stands behind Jesus. In her hands, she holds a very expensive alabaster jar of perfume.

It is well known how Mary makes her living, for there are few secrets in the small villages and towns of Galilee. But Mary has come to believe in the love and acceptance

An alabaster vase and a pottery vase from ancient Lebanon; dates unknown.
[Library of Congress LC-M32-7594]

preached by Jesus. Now, overcome with emotion, she bends down to pour the aromatic perfume on his feet. But she begins to sob before she can open the jar. Mary's tears flow freely and without shame, and her face is pressed close to the feet of the Nazarene, which are still dirty and coated in road dust from his walk to the Pharisee's house.

Mary's tears continue and mix with the perfume she applies to Jesus. She then dries his feet with her long hair, even as she kisses them as a sign of love and respect.

Jesus does nothing to stop her.

"Simon, I have something to tell you," Jesus says as Mary opens the alabaster jar and pours more perfume on his feet. The smell is enchanting and powerful, filling the room with its flowery sweetness.

"Tell me, teacher," Simon replies smoothly.

"Do you see this woman? I came into your house. You did not give me any water for my feet, but she wet my feet with her tears and wiped them with her hair. You did not give me a kiss, but this woman, from the time I entered, has not stopped kissing my feet," Jesus tells the Pharisee. "You did not put oil on my head, but she has poured perfume on my feet. Therefore, I tell you, her many sins have been forgiven—as her great love has shown. But whoever has been forgiven little loves little."

Jesus looks at Mary. She lifts her eyes to see his face. "Your sins are forgiven," Jesus tells her.

If Simon was looking for a chance to catch Jesus in a theological trap, now is the moment. Sins can be forgiven only through sacrificial offerings. In the eyes of the Pharisees, even baptisms performed in the Jordan River do not officially forgive sins. And now Jesus is saying that *he* has the authority to obliterate sin.

The other friends of Simon who have come to dinner this evening are dumbfounded by Jesus's words, particularly since he spoke them in the presence of such a prominent Pharisee. "Who is this who even forgives sins?" they ask one another.

"Your faith has saved you," Jesus tells Mary of Magdala. "Go in peace."

She goes, but not for long. Mary isn't selected by Jesus to serve as one of his twelve disciples, but she follows them as they travel, and she never returns to the life she once knew. At the end, Mary will be a powerful witness to the last days of Jesus of Nazareth.

CHAPTER 13

JOHN THE BAPTIST IS MURDERED

AD 27–29 ✦ MACHAERUS, OVERLOOKING THE DEAD SEA

FAR AWAY, IN THE DUNGEONS OF MACHAERUS, JOHN the Baptist waits. He has been imprisoned for two long years on this mountaintop in the middle of the desert. The dank cells of the prison have been carved into the rocky hillside, and, in fact, some are nothing more than caves. The floors, ceilings, and walls are impenetrable rock. There are no windows, and the only light comes through small slits in the thick wooden door. It is a place of solitude and silence, damp and chill, where hope is hard to maintain through month after month of sleeping on the ground, and the skin grows pale from never feeling the warmth of sunlight. It has been so long that John is beginning to doubt his initial faith in Jesus as the Messiah. He desperately wants to get word to Jesus and be reassured by him.

View of the hill Machaerus on which Herod's fortress was built. [dbajurin/123RF]

The months in isolation have given John time to reflect on his ministry. He is still a young man, not yet forty. But the longer he remains in prison, the more it appears that he might eventually be executed. His life's work has been to tell people about the coming of the Messiah, and he needs to know that it has not been in vain.

Now and then, John's disciples are allowed to visit him. He sends a message to Jesus with one of them: "Ask him," the Baptist says, "are you the one who is to come, or should we expect someone else?"

Weeks pass with no word. The journey from Machaerus to Galilee is just four days. John prays as he waits patiently for more news about Jesus.

Finally, he hears the shuffle of sandals outside the prison door. His disciples have returned, bringing with them some very specific words from Jesus. "He told us, 'Go back and report to John what you hear and see: The blind receive sight, the lame walk, those who have leprosy are cleansed, the deaf hear, the dead are raised, and the good news is proclaimed to the poor. Blessed is anyone who does not stumble on account of me.'"

John is relieved. This is the affirmation he was hoping to hear. Now he can finally find some semblance of peace as he languishes in prison. Jesus is once again claiming that he is the person John publicly proclaimed him to be: the Son of God.

But there's more. The eager disciples go on to tell John that Jesus not only alluded to his own virgin birth, as foretold by Scripture, but also extended a warm compliment to John as a reminder to stand strong. The moment came as Jesus was teaching to a crowd within earshot of John's disciples. In fact, they were just about to leave when Jesus made sure they heard these words: "What did you go out into the wilderness to see?" he asked the crowd in reference to John. "A reed swayed by the wind? A man dressed in fine clothes? No, those who wear fine clothes are in kings' palaces. Then what did you go out to see? A prophet? Yes, I tell you, and more than a prophet. This is the one about whom it is written: 'I will send my messenger ahead of you, who will prepare your way before you.'

"Truly I tell you, among those born of women, there has not risen anyone greater than John the Baptist."

✦　✦　✦　✦　✦

Another year passes. One night John the Baptist can hear that Antipas is having a party in his palace on this mountaintop. Antipas has invited the most powerful men in Galilee for a banquet. Men and women dine in separate halls, as is the custom. In the men's hall, Antipas calls for entertainment. His stepdaughter, Salome, enters and performs a solo dance. She is so beautiful that the men can't take their eyes off her. Antipas feels powerful and extravagant. "Ask me for anything you want, and I'll give it to you," he calls to the girl.

Salome is young and clever. She rushes from the room to find her mother for advice. "What shall I ask for?" Salome says.

"The head of John the Baptist," her mother replies.

John the Baptist hears the creak of his cell door swinging open. An executioner carrying a broad, sharpened sword enters alone. By the light of the moon, he forces John to his knees. The Baptist is resigned to his fate. The swordsman then raises his weapon high overhead and viciously brings it down.

John does not feel the weight of the heavy steel blade as it slices his head from his body.

The voice of one crying out in the wilderness is now silent.

Herodias has had her revenge against the Baptist for condemning her marriage. But if she and Antipas think that killing John will end the religious fervor now sweeping through Galilee, they are very wrong. John may have stirred strong emotions by cleansing believers of their sins, but another presence is challenging authority in ways never before seen or heard.

Machaerus as it looked in the 1920s. [Library of Congress]

CHAPTER 14

DEFEATED

APRIL, AD 29 ✦ GALILEE ✦ DAY

WITH EVERY PASSING DAY, JESUS'S LIFE IS MORE AND more in danger. Many Galileans believe he is the Christ. Because of this, the Roman authorities are paying close attention to Jesus. For under Roman law, a man who claims to be a king is guilty of rebellion against the emperor, a crime punishable by crucifixion. Knowing this, Jesus takes great care to no longer publicly confirm that he is the Christ.

The representatives of Rome, the Roman governor, Pontius Pilate, and Jewish administrator of Galilee, Herod Antipas, have not acted yet. So far, Jesus has shown himself to be a peaceful man. Other than the lone incident with the temple money changers, nothing he has done threatens them or their way of life. He has never once suggested that the people of Galilee rise up against Rome. So they are content to watch from afar—for the moment.

Roman writing materials, including an ink pot, oil lamp, seal, stylus, and wax tablet. From the Verulamium Museum in England. [The Bridgeman Art Library]

But the religious authorities feel differently. Led by the temple high priest, Caiaphas, the Pharisees and Sadducees see Jesus as a very real danger. To them, his preaching is a threat to their spiritual authority.

There is a second side to the religious leaders' objections to Jesus as well. He threatens their livelihood and wealth. Caiaphas, for example, has amassed his wealth partly through temple taxes—profits from the money changers and the temple concession for sacrificial lambs—so he has a great deal at stake.

These self-proclaimed men of God have devised a specific plan for handling Jesus: a quiet arrest, followed by a hasty execution.

But the religious leaders would be rendered impure if they murdered Jesus in cold blood. They cannot pay someone to run him through with a sword or to strangle him in his sleep. No, the Pharisees must play by traditional rules, and this means killing Jesus for a public violation of religious law.

Portrait of a Roman man holding a scroll, 1st century AD. [The Bridgeman Art Library]

In search of such an offense, a select team of Pharisees and scribes now travels from Jerusalem to Galilee to observe and listen to Jesus. They are men well versed in the Scriptures. If anyone can find fault with Jesus, they can.

Or so the religious leaders believe.

Things go wrong from the start. The Pharisees and Sadducees are frustrated at every turn, for Jesus is a spiritual and intellectual rival unlike any they have ever faced. Despite their best efforts to weaken his movement through public interrogation, Jesus outwits them at every turn, and his popularity continues to soar. The people of Galilee begin to monitor Jesus's travels so closely that they anticipate where he is going and then race ahead to wait for him. Stories of Jesus turning water into wine and making the lame walk and the blind see have so electrified the region that it is now commonplace for almost anyone with an ailment to seek him out, even if that means being carried for miles to await his appearance. Indeed, the Pharisees themselves witness a puzzling event, as Jesus apparently heals a man's severely withered hand on the Sabbath—an act which the Pharisees promptly and publicly condemn as a violation of religious law.

Jesus uses logic and words of Scripture to upend their arguments. One spring day, he and his disciples purchase a meal in the marketplace and prepare to enjoy it. Soon a circle of well-dressed Pharisees gathers around to condemn them for not engaging in the ceremonial washing of the hands. This ritual also includes a premeal cleansing of cups, plates, and cutlery, and is far more suited to the

temple courts than a Galilean fishing village. Of course, the famished disciples are in no mood to indulge in such a lengthy process.

A Pharisee taunts Jesus: "Why do your disciples break the tradition of the elders? They don't wash their hands before they eat!"

Jesus is calm. He begins by answering a question with a question, a technique he often uses. "And why do you break the command of God for the sake of your tradition?"

The Pharisees move closer to the group. A crowd of curious onlookers gathers just behind them. There is now a tight ring around Jesus and his disciples.

The Pharisees hope that Jesus will now utter words of blasphemy and heresy. If he does, he can be condemned. What they want to hear most is a claim of divinity, a public proclamation by Jesus that he is the Son of God—not an earthly king, but one exalted above the angels and seated on the throne with God.

That would be enough to have Jesus stoned to death.

Jesus stands to address the Pharisees. The people of Galilee press closer to hear what he will say. These simple craftsmen and fishermen look poor and tattered in comparison with the Pharisees. Jesus, their fellow Galilean, is dressed just as they are, wearing a simple square robe over his tunic.

"You hypocrites! Isaiah was right when he prophesied about you," Jesus says, looking directly at the Pharisees and Sadducees. He then quotes from the Scripture: "'These people honor me with their lips, but their hearts are far from me. They worship me in vain; their teachings are merely human rules.'"

Group of tiny Roman objects made of alabaster used for makeup and writing, including boxes, vials, comb, papyrus stand, mirror, scribe, and tray. These were tomb furnishings, meant to be buried with a body for use in the afterlife. [The Bridgeman Art Library]

Jesus is fearless. The force of his words carries out over the crowd. Even though the Pharisees have come here to judge him, the tone of Jesus's voice makes it clear that it is *he* who is judging them. "You have let go of the commands of God and are holding on to human traditions," he scolds his accusers.

Before they can reply, Jesus turns to the crowd and says, "Listen to me, everyone, and understand this. Nothing outside a person can defile them by going into them. Rather, it is what comes out of a person that defiles them."

The Pharisees walk away before Jesus can further undermine

their authority. The remaining crowds make it impossible for the disciples to eat in peace, so Jesus leads them into a nearby house to dine without being disturbed.

But the disciples are unsettled. They have heard and absorbed so much of what Jesus has said in their year together and have been witness to many strange and powerful events that they do not understand. They are simple men and do not comprehend why Jesus is so intent on humiliating the all-powerful Pharisees. This escalating religious battle can only end poorly for Jesus—and the disciples know it.

Peter speaks up. "Explain the parable to us," he asks, knowing that Jesus never says anything publicly without a reason.

Jesus says, "Don't you see that whatever enters the mouth goes into the stomach and then out of the body? But the things that come out of a person's mouth come from the heart, and these defile them. For out of the heart come evil thoughts—murder, adultery, sexual immorality, theft, false testimony, slander. These are what defile a person."

CHAPTER 15

"WHO DO PEOPLE SAY I AM?"

APRIL, AD 29 ✦ GALILEE ✦ DAY

JUDAS ISCARIOT IS AMONG THOSE LISTENING TO THE words of Jesus. He is the lone disciple who was not raised in Galilee, making him a conspicuous outsider in the group. There is no denying this. He wears the same robes and sandals, covers his head to keep off the sun, and carries a walking stick to defend himself from the wild dogs of Galilee, just like the rest of the disciples. But he is from the south, not the north. Every time he opens his mouth to speak, his accent reminds the disciples that he is different.

Now Jesus's words push him farther away from the group. For Judas is also a thief. Taking advantage of his role as treasurer, he steals regularly from the disciples' meager finances. Rather than allow Jesus to be anointed with precious perfumes by his admirers, Judas has insisted that those vials of perfume be sold and the profits placed in the group's communal moneybag so that he might steal the money for his own use. Judas's acts of thievery have remained a secret, and like all thieves, he carries the private burden of his sin.

Judas apparently believes in the teachings of Jesus and certainly basks in Jesus's celebrity. But his desire for material wealth overrides any spirituality. He puts his own needs above those of Jesus and the other disciples.

For a price, Judas Iscariot is capable of doing anything.

Frustrated by their inability to trap Jesus, but also believing they have enough evidence to arrest him, the Pharisees and Sadducees return to Jerusalem to make their report. And while it may seem as if Jesus is unbothered by their attention, the truth is that the pressure is weighing on him enormously. Even before their visit, Jesus had hoped to take refuge in a solitary place for a time of reflection and prayer. Now he flees Galilee, taking the disciples with him. They walk thirty-four miles north, into the kingdom ruled by Antipas's brother Philip, toward the city of Caesarea Philippi. The people there are pagans who worship the god Pan, that deity with the hindquarters and horns of a goat and the face of a man. No one there cares if Jesus says he is the Christ, nor will the authorities question him about Scripture.

Summer is approaching. The two-day journey follows a well-traveled Roman road on the east side of the Hula Valley. Jesus and his disciples keep a sharp eye out for the bears and bandits that can do harm, but otherwise their trip is peaceful. Actually, this is like a vacation for Jesus and the disciples, and they aren't too many miles

up the road before Jesus feels refreshed enough to stop and relax in the sun.

"Who do the crowds say I am?" Jesus asks the disciples.

"Some say John the Baptist; others say Elijah; and still others, that one of the prophets of long ago has come back to life," come the replies.

It is often this way when they travel—Jesus teaching on the go or prompting intellectual debate by throwing out a random question.

"But what about you?" Jesus inquires. "Who do you say I am?"

Simon speaks up. "You are the Messiah, the Son of the living God."

Jesus agrees. "Blessed are you, Simon son of Jonah, for this was not revealed to you by flesh and blood, but by my father in heaven," he praises the impulsive fisherman.

"Don't tell anyone," Jesus adds as a reminder that a public revelation will lead to his arrest by the Romans. They may be leaving the power of the Jewish authorities behind for a short while, but Caesarea Philippi is just as Roman as Rome itself.

But if the disciples think that Jesus has shared his deepest secret yet, they are wrong. "The Son of Man must suffer many things and be rejected by the elders, the chief priests, and the teachers of the law," Jesus goes on to explain.

This doesn't make sense to the disciples. If Jesus is the Christ, then he will one day rule the land. But how can he do so without the backing of the religious authorities?

And if that isn't confusing enough, Jesus adds another statement, one that will be a source of argument through the ages.

"He must be killed," Jesus promises the disciples, speaking of himself as the Son of God, "and on the third day be raised to life."

The disciples have no idea what this means.

Nor do they know that Jesus of Nazareth, the teacher who inspires them, has less than a year to live.

CHAPTER 16

THE FEAST OF TABERNACLES

OCTOBER, AD 29 ✦ JERUSALEM ✦ DAY

IT IS THE TIME OF THE FEAST OF TABERNACLES, OR
Sukkoth, one of the great celebrations on the Jewish religious calendar. As at Passover, pilgrims by the thousands
travel to Jerusalem. On this occasion, the Jews commemorate
forty years of wandering in the desert, searching for the Promised Land. It is also a harvest celebration.

Pontius Pilate, his wife, Claudia, and three thousand soldiers are arriving in Jerusalem. Pilate's military caravan has set
out from the seaside fortress of Caesarea. The Roman governor
makes the trip to Jerusalem three times a year for the Jewish
festivals. The sixty-mile journey takes them south along the
Mediterranean, on a paved Roman road. After an overnight
stop, the route turns inward, onto a dirt road across the Plains
of Sharon and on up through the mountains to Jerusalem.

The Jewish Religious Year

Daily life for the Jews in Galilee and Judea revolved around holy days and religious celebrations. Below is the calendar, which starts with September when the Jewish year begins. The name of the month as transliterated from Hebrew is underlined. It is followed by the corresponding names of the months in the Western calendar. Underneath the months are the approximate dates and names of the holy days.

TISHRI (September–October)
- 1, 2   Rosh Hashanah (New Year)
- 3   Tzom Gedaliahu (Fast of Gedaliah)
- 10   Yom Kippur (Day of Atonement)
- 15–21   Sukkoth (Feast of Tabernacles)
- 22   Shemini Atzereth (Eighth Day of the Solemn Assembly)
- 23   Simchas Torah (Rejoicing of the Law)

HESHVAN or MARHESHVAN (October–November)

KISLEV (November–December)
- 25   Hanukkah (Feast of Dedication) begins

TEBET (December–January)
  2–3 Hanukkah ends
    10 Asara be-Tebet (Fast of Tebet)

SHEBAT (January–February)
    15 Tu-bi-Shebat (New Year of the
          Trees)

ADAR (February–March)
    13 Ta'anit Esther (Fast of Esther)
14, 15 Purim (Feast of Lots)

NISAN (March–April)
15–22 Pesach (Passover)

IYAR (April–May)
    18 Lag b'Omer (33rd Day of the
          Omer Counting)

SIVAN (May–June)
  6, 7 Shabuoth (Feast of Weeks, or
          Pentecost)

TAMMUZ (June–July)
    17 Shiva Asar b'Tammuz (Fast of
          Tammuz)

AB (July–August)
     9 Tishah-b'Ab (Fast of Ab)

ELUL (August–September)

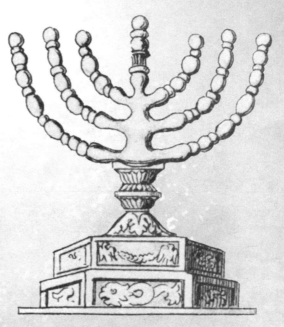

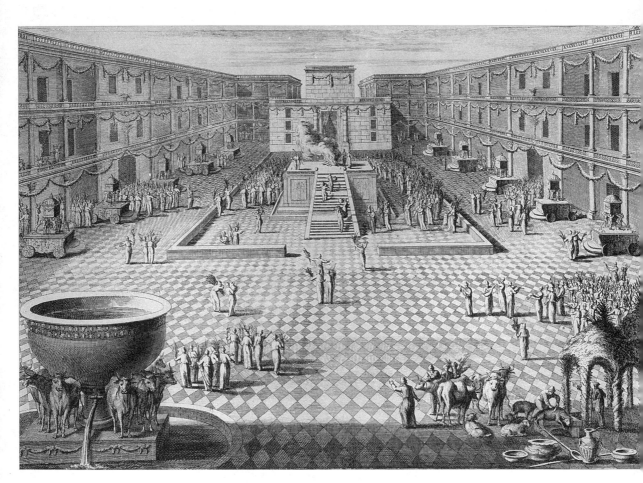

Representation of the celebration of the Feast of Tabernacles in the temple in Jerusalem. French 18th-century engraving. [The Bridgeman Art Library]

Pilate intends to lend a dominant Roman presence to the Feast of Tabernacles, as he does for each important celebration. Pilate has little patience for Jewish ways. Nor does he think the Jews are loyal to Rome. The governor walks a fine line during these festivals: if the Jews revolt—which they are likely to do when they gather by the hundreds of thousands—he will take the blame, but if he cracks down too hard, he could be recalled to Rome for disobeying Tiberius's order that these people be treated as a "sacred trust."

Thus Pilate endures the festival weeks. He and Claudia lodge themselves in Herod the Great's lavish palace and venture out only when absolutely necessary.

To the Jewish people, Pilate is a villain. They think him "spiteful and angry" and speak of "his venality, his violence, his thefts, his assaults, his abusive behavior, his frequent executions of untried prisoners, and his endless savage ferocity."

Yet one of their own is just as guilty.

✦ ✦ ✦ ✦ ✦

Pontius Pilate cannot rule the Jewish people without the help of Joseph Caiaphas, the high priest and leader of the Jewish judicial court known as the Sanhedrin. Caiaphas is a master politician and knows that Emperor Tiberius not only believes it important to uphold the Jewish traditions, but is also keeping the hot-tempered Pilate on a very short leash. Pilate may be in charge of Judea, but it is Caiaphas who oversees the day-to-day running of Jerusalem.

Prior to Caiaphas, high priests were puppets of Rome, easily replaced for acts of insubordination. But Caiaphas, a member of the Sadducee sect, has developed a simple and brilliant technique to remain in power: stay out of Rome's business.

Rome, in turn, usually stays out of the temple's business.

This lets Pilate keep his job and increases Caiaphas's power.

In fact, Pilate and Caiaphas are more alike than they are different. Pilate was born into the wealthy equestrian class of Romans, and Caiaphas was born into a centuries-long lineage of wealthy temple priests. Both men are middle aged and married. When Pilate is in Jerusalem, he lives a few hundred yards away from Caiaphas in a fancy Upper City palace. And they consider themselves devout men, though they worship far different deities.

As Pilate enters the city, Jesus's disciples are traveling to Jerusalem. They see this festival as the chance for Jesus to proclaim his divinity. In fact, they try to give him a piece of advice—something they've never done before. "Go to Judea," they beg before setting out. "No one who wants to become a public figure acts in secret. Since you are doing these things, show yourself to the world."

"My time is not yet here," Jesus answers. "For you any time will do. The world cannot hate you, but it hates me because I testify that its works are evil. You go to the festival. I am not going up to this festival, because my time has not yet fully come."

When the religious leaders see the disciples enter the city without Jesus, they are immediately frustrated—once again, he appears

Remaining interior courtyard of Pontius Pilate's palace in Jerusalem. Contemporary photograph. [Shutterstock]

to be getting the best of them. "Where is that man?" the Pharisees ask one another, studying the faces in the crowds filling the temple courts. "Where is that man?"

Rumors about Jesus swirl as the festival begins. For days, speculation spreads through the city. No one has an answer about where Jesus is, not even his own disciples. Then, halfway through the eight-day festival, Jesus slips quietly into the temple courts. Within moments, pilgrims surround him, listening in amazement as he shares his insights about God.

"Isn't this the man they are trying to kill?" ask some in the crowd.

"Have the authorities really concluded that he is the Messiah?" ask others.

This idea is met with doubt because it is hard to imagine that the new king, the savior, would come from a backwater province like Galilee. Instead, he should be from Bethlehem, the city of David, as told by the prophets.

Jesus teaches in the temple courts for the rest of the festival. "I am the light of the world. Whoever follows me will never walk in darkness, but will have the light of life," he tells the crowds. "I am going away," Jesus adds. "Where I go you cannot come."

And soon after that, he leaves. As pilgrims travel back to their homes, whether in Egypt, Syria, Galilee, Greece, Gaul, or Rome, they talk about Jesus. Many now believe that he is indeed the Christ. Others are not sure, but they have heard his pronouncements that he was sent by God, and they desperately want to put their faith in him.

For whether or not they believe that Jesus is the Christ, Jews everywhere long for the coming of a messiah. When that moment arrives, Rome will be defeated and their lives will be free of taxation and want. No longer will soldiers loyal to Rome be allowed to corral Jews like cattle, then stab and beat them until the gutters of their holy city are choked with Jewish blood. This hope is like a lifeline, giving them courage in the face of Rome's unrelenting cruelty.

Some pilgrims are waiting for a verbal pronouncement from Jesus: "I am the Christ." Others are waiting for the fulfillment of the prophecy—the moment that Jesus rides into Jerusalem on a donkey. Then and only then will they be sure that he is the one true Christ. "See, your king comes to you, righteous and victorious, lowly and riding on a donkey, on a colt, the foal of a donkey," the prophet Zechariah predicted five hundred years ago. "He will proclaim peace to the nations. His rule will extend from sea to sea and from the River to the ends of the earth."

✦　✦　✦　✦　✦

[NEXT PAGES] *A model of the Hasmonean Palace in Jerusalem as it might have looked in AD 66.* [The Bridgeman Art Library]

Pontius Pilate is now safely back in Caesarea, destined not to return to Jerusalem until April and the Passover celebration. Jesus has left Galilee. Witnesses say he is performing miracles once again. In one startling account from the town of Bethany, a man named Lazarus came back from the dead. He had died four days earlier and had already been laid in the tomb when Jesus ordered that the stone covering the entrance be rolled away. He called out to Lazarus, and the man walked out of the tomb.

"Here is this man performing many signs," a Pharisee says. "If we let him go on like this, everyone will believe in him, and then the Romans will come and take away both our place and our nation."

Caiaphas agrees. "You do not realize that it is better for you that one man die for the people than that the whole nation perish."

Nothing more needs to be said.

✦　✦　✦　✦　✦

At the age of thirty-six, Jesus is clever enough to act out any prophecy. His knowledge of Scripture and understanding of faith are encyclopedic.

The prophets have been very specific about the way that the king of the Jews would be born and live his life; they are just as clear about how he will die.

He will be falsely accused of crimes he did not commit.

He will be beaten.

He will be spat upon.

He will be stripped, and soldiers will throw dice for his clothing.

He will be crucified, with nails driven through his hands and feet.

And he will die during Passover.

Five months have passed. It is now approaching Passover. Pontius Pilate is in Jerusalem settled into Herod the Great's palace. Herod Antipas arrives in the city and stays just a block away at the Hasmonean palace. At the same time, Caiaphas prepares for the biggest festival of the year at his palace home in the Upper City.

Passover week is about to begin.

The disciples begin the search for a donkey.

Jesus of Nazareth has six days to live.

BOOK III

THE LAST WEEK
DAY by DAY

CHAPTER 17

THE PASSOVER JOURNEY BEGINS

FRIDAY/SATURDAY, MARCH 30/31, AD 30 ✦ BETHANY

"WE ARE GOING UP TO JERUSALEM," JESUS TELLS HIS disciples as they prepare to depart for Passover. "The Son of Man will be delivered over to the chief priests and the teachers of the law. They will condemn him to death and will turn him over to the Gentiles to be mocked and flogged and crucified. On the third day he will be raised to life."

But if those words disturb the disciples, they don't show it. For theirs has been a journey of many months, rather than the mere days of most pilgrims. After the Feast of Tabernacles five months ago, Jesus and the disciples did not return to Galilee. Instead, they began a roundabout trip. First stop, the village of Ephraim, only fifteen miles north of Jerusalem. From there they traveled as a group away from Jerusalem, to the border of

Samaria and Galilee. And then when it came time for Passover, they turned in the opposite direction and marched south along the River Jordan, joining the long caravans of pilgrims going to the holy city.

The disciples now jockey for position during the walk to Jerusalem. James and John ask Jesus if they can be his principal assistants in the new regime, requesting that "one of us sit at your right and the other at your left in your glory." Upon hearing this, the other ten are furious. They have followed Jesus as a group for more than two years, giving up their jobs and leaving their wives and whatever semblance of a normal life they had. All the disciples hope they will reap the glory that will come after the new Messiah overthrows the Romans. Peter is so sure that Jesus is going to use military might that he is making plans to purchase a sword.

But Jesus has no plans to wage war and no plans to form a new government. Rather than scold James and John, he calmly deflects their request. He then calls the disciples together, instructing them to focus on serving others rather than fighting for position. "For even the Son of Man did not come to be served, but to serve, and to give his life as a ransom for many," he tells them.

Once again, Jesus is predicting his death. And yet the disciples are so focused on the glorious moment when he will reveal that he is the Christ that they can't hear that he is telling them he will soon die. There will be no overthrow of the Romans. There will be no new government.

The disciples' willful ignorance is understandable. Jesus often

speaks in parables, and the excitement surrounding him is now phenomenal. The love and adoration being bestowed upon Jesus makes any talk of death unbelievable. The thick crowds of pilgrims treat Jesus like royalty, hanging on his every word and greeting him with enthusiastic awe. In the village of Jericho, two blind men call out to Jesus, referring to him as "Lord, Son of David"—a designation that could only be applied to the Christ. The disciples are encouraged when Jesus does nothing to rebuke the blind men.

Jerusalem is just a forty-minute walk from the village of Bethany, where they stop for the night. They stay at the home of Lazarus and his sisters Mary and Martha. This will be their base throughout Passover week, and Jesus and the disciples plan to return here most nights for the promise of a hot meal and easy rest.

Sabbath, the seventh day of the week, begins at sundown on Friday and continues through sundown on Saturday. The Jews call it Shabbat. It is a day of mandatory rest in the Jewish religion, commemorating the idea that after creating the universe, God rested. Jesus and the apostles spend the time quietly, preparing for the week to come.

The serenity of Lazarus's home provides Jesus and the disciples with relief from the road. Hospitality is a vital aspect of Jewish society, dating back to the days when the patriarch Abraham treated all guests as if they were angels in disguise, offering them lavish meals of veal, butter, bread, and milk. So it is that the spacious home of Lazarus, with its large courtyard and thick door to keep out intruders at night, is not just a refuge for Jesus and the disciples, but also a vibrant link to the roots of their Jewish faith.

Stone statue of Martha, sister of Lazarus and Mary; carved in the 16th century, Church of St. Madeleine, Troyes, France. [The Bridgeman Art Library]

Martha and Mary dote on Jesus, though in opposite ways. Martha, the older of the two, is constantly fussing over him. Mary, meanwhile, is enthralled. She sits at his feet and sometimes shows her respect by anointing them with perfumed oil. In her own way, each woman gives him comfort. They see to it that Jesus and the disciples remove their sandals and wash their feet upon returning each evening, so that any impurities or infections might be cleansed. A stepped pool in the basement offers Jesus a place to bathe and change into his other set of clothes. Martha and Mary will wash the dusty clothes. And of course, Jesus and the others will wash their hands before sitting down to eat.

During Passover week, Martha and Mary serve two meals a day. Dinner is fresh bread, olive oil, soup, and sometimes beef or salted fish washed down with homemade wine. Breakfast features bread and fruit—though dried, instead of fresh, because melons and pomegranates are out of season. As Jesus learned on the road yesterday morning, the local fig and date orchards will not ripen for months to come.

Even though Lazarus truly enjoys being with him, Jesus's presence means much more than that. This is a man whom Lazarus trusts, reveres, and indeed, to whom he owes his very life.

Vessel for ritual hand washing before eating, inscribed with the prayer said while washing. Made of brass with colored glass; no date. [The Bridgeman Art Library]

CHAPTER 18

THE TRIUMPHAL ENTRANCE INTO JERUSALEM

SUNDAY, APRIL 1, AD 30 ✦ OUTSIDE JERUSALEM

JESUS AND HIS DISCIPLES SET OUT ALONG THE DUSTY dirt road from Bethany that is clogged with Passover pilgrims eager to enter the walls of Jerusalem. The day is sunny, as it is so often this time of year. The travelers push past date palm plantations and small farming villages where fruit orchards, vineyards, and olive trees grow alongside irrigated fields of vegetables.

Before they enter the gates of Jerusalem, the travelers stop for their ritual *mikvah*, or bath, to purify themselves. Anticipating the smell of roast lamb that will hang over Jerusalem as the Passover feasts are being cooked in ovens, the pilgrims count their money, worrying about how they will pay for that feast and the inevitable taxes they will incur in the city. Despite the sore feet and aching legs from walking mile after rugged mile, the magnetic pull of Jerusalem is transforming the travelers. Their thoughts are no longer set on their farms back home and the barley crop that must be harvested immediately upon their return, but on holiness and purity.

Soon they will ascend the hill known as the Mount of Olives and look down upon Jerusalem in all its glory. The temple will gleam white and gold, and the mighty walls of the Temple Mount will astound them, as always. Its sheer magnificence will remind them that they have arrived at the center of Jewish life.

As they near Jerusalem, Jesus selects two disciples and gives them

A mikvah, *or ritual bath. This one is at the ruins of Herod the Great's fortress at Masada.* [Corbis]

a special task. "Go to the village ahead of you," Jesus orders them, "and at once you will find a donkey tied there, with her colt by her. Untie them. If anyone says anything to you, say that the Lord needs them, and he will send them right away."

Later, just on the other side of Bethpage, the town where they found the donkey, the two disciples stand waiting. One holds the bridle of the donkey. A disciple removes his square cloak and lays it across the animal's bare back as an improvised saddle. The other disciples remove their cloaks and lay them on the ground in an act of submission, forming a carpet on which the donkey can walk. Following this example, many of the pilgrims remove their own cloaks and lay them on the ground. Others gather palm fronds or snap branches off olive and cypress trees and wave them with delight.

This is the sign everyone has been waiting for. This is the fulfillment of Zechariah's prophecy. "Blessed is the king!" shouts a disciple.

The people join in, exalting Jesus and crying out to him. "Hosanna," they chant. "Hosanna in the highest."

Jesus rides on the donkey, and the people bow down.

"O Lord, save us," they implore, thankful that the Christ has finally come to rescue them. "O Lord, grant us success. Blessed is he who comes in the name of the Lord." The words of thanksgiving are from a psalm sung at Passover. This is the moment for which these simple peasants have waited so long. Of all the thousands of pilgrims who set out from Galilee, these are the lucky few who can

tell their children and their children's children that they witnessed the grand moment when Jesus the Christ rode triumphantly into Jerusalem.

But not everyone bows down. A group of Pharisees has been waiting for Jesus, and they now look on with disgust. They call out to him, giving Jesus one last chance to avoid a charge of blasphemy. "Teacher," they yell, "rebuke your disciples!"

But Jesus refuses. "I tell you," he informs the Pharisees, "if they keep quiet, the stones will cry out."

Others who have heard that Jesus is near have run out from Jerusalem, spreading palm branches across his path. This is a traditional sign of triumph and glory.

The donkey stops atop the

The Golden Gate leading from the Mount of Olives to the Temple Mount. It was blocked up by the Ottomans in 1530.
[The Bridgeman Art Library]

Mount of Olives. Jesus takes it all in. Tents cover the hillside where poor Galileans camp during Passover. Jerusalem calls out to him from just across the small Kidron Valley, and the temple gleams in the midday sun. Throngs of pilgrims line the path winding down into the valley. The mud and limestone trail is remarkably steep, and Jesus will have to use great caution to guide the donkey downhill without getting thrown.

This is his day. Jesus's whole life has pointed to this moment when he will ride forth to stake his claim to the title "king of the Jews."

Suddenly, Jesus begins to weep. Perhaps it's the thought of spending a last week with his good friends Lazarus, Mary, and Martha. Maybe he foresees the eventual destruction of this great city. Or perhaps Jesus looks on Jerusalem knowing that his own pageantry will be short-lived. For he has powerful enemies within the city walls.

In his moment of triumph, Jesus is experiencing agony. He has long strategized about the words he will say at Passover and the effect they will have on his followers, both old and new. He knows that his claims of being a king will lead to his crucifixion. He will be sacrificed, just as surely as those countless Passover lambs. It is just a matter of when.

It is time to go. As the hosannas rain down on all sides and the Pharisees look on from a place nearby with their usual veiled contempt, Jesus coaxes the donkey forward. Step by careful step, the two descend the Mount of Olives, cross the Kidron Valley through a tunnel of worshippers, and ride majestically up the hill into the great and golden city.

Jesus is almost casual, dismounting from the donkey and walking straight up the great steps into the temple courts. He has not come here to teach, but to be a pilgrim just like any man from Galilee, observing the sights and smells and sounds of the temple during Passover week.

Roman soldiers are posted throughout the Court of the Gentiles, and the temple guards no doubt take note of Jesus and the people who crowd around him. But none of them make a move to arrest Jesus. Apprehending such a beloved public figure might cause a riot. With Jews pouring into Jerusalem by the hundreds of thousands, even the smallest confrontation could quickly get out of hand. The soldiers and guards are armed, but their numbers are minuscule in comparison with the number of pilgrims. Anyone trying to take Jesus into custody could be overwhelmed by the peasant hordes. Anger about the injustice of arresting such a peaceful man would blend with their simmering rage about heavy taxation.

It is late afternoon when Jesus departs the temple courts in order to get back to Bethany before nightfall. Jesus and the disciples retrace their steps back out of Jerusalem, past the tent camps on the Mount of Olives—where trampled palm leaves and olive branches still litter the dirt road. Even though the crowds have made it clear that they wanted him to be their king and treated his arrival as a prelude to his coronation, Jesus has neither said nor done anything to lead Caiaphas or Pilate to believe that he is plotting a rebellion.

CHAPTER 19

"HOSANNA"

**MONDAY, APRIL 2, AD 30 ✦
JERUSALEM ✦ MORNING**

IT IS DAWN. JESUS AND THE DISCIPLES ARE ALREADY ON the move, walking purposefully from Bethany back into Jerusalem. The pandemonium of yesterday's jubilant entry into that city still rings in Jesus's ear. He was adored by the people as "Jesus, the prophet from Nazareth in Galilee" when he dismounted at the city gates. It was a coronation of sorts, a celebration. But to the authorities, the spectacle was cause for great concern. Jerusalem hasn't seen such a moment since Jewish rebels tried to capture the city in 4 BC and again ten years later. Those rebels, of course, paid for their actions with their lives.

Jesus knows this, just as he knows that the Roman governor, Pontius Pilate, and the Jewish high priest, Caiaphas, are constantly on the lookout for rebels and subversives. He is well aware that each received at least some word from spies and subordinates that Jesus had ridden into the city on a donkey, stirring up the Passover crowds.

Jesus spots a fig tree. He and the twelve disciples are just outside Bethany, and Jesus has had little to eat this morning. He walks alone to the tree, hoping to pluck a piece of fruit, even though he knows that figs are out of season. Jesus searches the twisted branches, but sees only leaves. Jesus is annoyed at the tree. "May no one ever eat fruit from you again," he says.

The outburst is uncharacteristic, and the disciples take note.

Once again, the group walks into Jerusalem and straight to the temple. It has been three years since Jesus turned over the money changers' tables. No longer an unknown figure, Jesus of Nazareth is now famous. His every movement is watched, as the Pharisees wait for the vital slipup that will allow them to make an arrest. Pilgrims cluster around Jesus, too, including parents with their children in tow, just like Mary and Joseph with the young Jesus so many years ago. A substantial number of the crowd today are followers of Jesus.

The little children begin cheering for Jesus. "Hosanna to the Son of David," calls out a child.

And then, as if it were a game, another child calls out the same thing. Soon, some in the crowd beg to be healed, right there in the temple. The Pharisees, as always, are watching. "Do you hear what these children are saying?" the chief priests and scribes call out indignantly to Jesus.

More hosannas ring throughout the temple courts, shouted again and again by children.

An ancient fig tree in a valley outside of Jerusalem. Drawing in ink by James Tissot, 19th century. [The Bridgeman Art Library]

"Do you hear what these people are saying?" the chief priests repeat.

"'From the lips of children and infants, you, Lord, have called forth your praise,'" Jesus tells them, quoting from David.

The religious leaders know the psalm well. It is a call for God to bask in the adoration of the children, then to rise up and strike hard at the powers of darkness who stand against him.

If the Pharisees' interpretation is correct, Jesus is actually comparing them to the forces of evil.

But still they don't motion for Jesus to be arrested. Nor do they try to stop him as he leaves the temple, trailed by his disciples.

The sun is now setting, and the first cooking fires are being lit on the Mount of Olives. Jesus and the disciples once again make the long walk back to Bethany. For now, he is a free man.

Six hundred years ago, when Jeremiah prophesied that the temple would be destroyed, he was punished by being lowered into an empty well. Jeremiah sank up to his waist in mud and was left to die.

But the time of Jesus is different. He is not a lone man, but a revolutionary with a band of disciples and growing legion of followers. His outbursts in the temple were an aggressive act against the religious leaders rather than a passive prediction that it would one day fall. Jesus is now openly antagonistic toward temple authorities.

At his home in the wealthy Upper City in Jerusalem, Caiaphas hears accounts of the temple crowds' responses to Jesus. He realizes more fully just how dangerous Jesus has become.

The threat must be squelched. As the temple's high priest and the most powerful Jewish authority in the world, Caiaphas is bound by religious law to immediately take extreme measures against Jesus. "If a prophet, or one who foretells by dreams, appears among you and announces to you a sign or wonder," reads the Book of Deuteronomy, "that prophet or dreamer must be put to death for inciting rebellion against the Lord your God."

Caiaphas knows that Jesus is playing a clever game by using the crowds as a tool to prevent his arrest. This is a game that Caiaphas plans to win. But to avoid the risk of becoming impure, he must move before sundown on Friday and the start of Passover.

This is the biggest week of the year for Caiaphas. He has an extraordinary number of obligations and administrative tasks that must be tended to if the Passover celebration is to come off smoothly. Rome is watching him closely through the eyes of Pontius Pilate, and any sort of failure on the part of Caiaphas during this most vital festival might lead to his dismissal.

But nothing matters more than silencing Jesus.

Time is running out. Passover starts in four short days.

CHAPTER 20

"RENDER UNTO CAESAR . . ."

TUESDAY, APRIL 3, AD 30 ✦ JERUSALEM ✦ MORNING

D AWN BREAKS. THE COUNTDOWN TO PASSOVER CON-
tinues as the citizens of Bethany are stirring. Inside Lazarus's home, Jesus and his disciples wash their hands and
eat their daily bread before setting out for another day in the
temple courts.

The group soon falls in alongside a line of travelers. Today
Jesus will teach in the temple courts, and he has prepared a
number of parables that will explain difficult theological issues
in ways that even the most unread listener can understand.

"Rabbi, look," exclaims a disciple as they walk past the fig
tree that Jesus searched for fruit yesterday. Its roots are shriv-
eled. "How did the fig tree wither so quickly?" the disciple
asks.

"Truly I tell you, if you have faith and do not doubt, not only can you do what was done to the fig tree, but also you can say to this mountain, 'Go, throw yourself into the sea,' and it will be done. If you believe, you will receive whatever you ask for in prayer," Jesus responds.

The disciples will marvel at what happened to that simple tree for years to come. They will write about it with awe, even decades from now, and quote the two-sentence response of Jesus.

As they draw close to Jerusalem, Jesus knows that a drama will unfold. He could sense it yesterday, when the religious leaders hovered at the fringe of every crowd, watching him intently as he

Sandals found at the excavation site in Masada, Israel, from the 1st century AD. [The Bridgeman Art Library]

interacted with his followers. These priests and Pharisees wear robes that are even more resplendent than normal this week, choosing their most colorful and expensive garments as a way of setting themselves apart from the drably dressed pilgrims. The priestly robes are a reminder that they are vital members of the temple, not mere visitors.

Jesus, meanwhile, still clothes himself like an average Galilean. He wears his seamless tunic, and over it, a simple robe. Sandals protect his feet from sharp pebbles and sticks as he walks, but do little to keep off the dust. So the walk from Bethany down into Jerusalem often gives him an unwashed appearance in comparison to the Pharisees, many of whom have bathing facilities and ritual pools in their nearby homes. And while his accent might sound country within the confines of the city of Jerusalem, Jesus does nothing to hide his native tongue. If anything, it works to his advantage, for it so often leads the religious leaders to underestimate him as just another pilgrim from Galilee.

Jesus and the disciples pass through the city gates. Their movements are now being closely tracked by the Roman spies and religious authorities, so their arrival is noted immediately. Jerusalem has grown louder and more festive with every passing day, as pilgrims continue to arrive from throughout the world. Voices speaking in Greek, Aramaic, Latin, Egyptian, and Hebrew now fill the air. The bleating of lambs is another constant, as shepherds bring tens of thousands of the small animals into the city to be sacrificed on Friday.

Jesus enters the temple courts. He selects a spot in the shaded awnings of Solomon's Porch and begins to teach.

Jesus tells a parable about a wealthy landowner and his troublesome tenants. The summation is a line stating that the religious leaders will lose their authority and be replaced by others whose belief is more genuine.

Then Jesus tells a second parable about heaven, comparing it to a wedding, with God as the father of the groom, preparing a luxurious banquet for his son's guests. Again, the religious leaders are the subject of the final line, a barb about a guest who shows up poorly dressed and is then bound hand and foot and thrown from the ceremony. "For many are invited," Jesus says of heaven, "but few are chosen."

A new group of temple priests has been sent to challenge Jesus. Aware that they're unlikely to catch him in a theological misstatement, they now try to trick Jesus using politics. "What is your opinion?" they ask. "Is it right to pay the imperial tax to Caesar or not?"

Portrait of Augustus Caesar on a Roman coin from the 1st century BC.
[The Bridgeman Art Library]

"Why are you trying to trap me?" Jesus seethes. He asks for someone to hand him a denarius. "Whose image is this?" he asks, holding up the coin. "And whose inscription?"

"Caesar's," they answer.

"So give back to Caesar what is Caesar's," Jesus tells them. "And to God what is God's."

Again, the crowd is awed. Although Caesar is a feared name, Jesus has put Rome in its place without directly offending it. The brilliance of these words will last throughout the ages.

Having failed in their mission, the group leaves. They are soon replaced by the Sadducees, a wealthy and more liberal temple sect who count Caiaphas among their numbers. Once again, they try to trick Jesus with a religious riddle, and once again they fail.

Soon the Pharisees step forward to take their turn. "Teacher," asks their leader, a man known for being an expert in the law, "which is the greatest commandment in the Law?"

Under the teachings of the Pharisees, there are

Julius Caesar, a 19th-century engraving.
[The Bridgeman Art Library]

613 religious statutes. Even though each carries a designation, marking it as either great or little, the fact remains that all must be followed. Asking Jesus to select one is a clever way of pushing him into a corner, making him defend his choice.

But Jesus does not choose from one of the established laws. Instead, he articulates a new one: "Love the Lord your God with all your heart and with all your soul and with all your mind. This is the first and greatest commandment."

The Pharisees stand silent. How could anyone argue with that? Then Jesus goes on to add a second law: "Love your neighbor as yourself. All the Law and the Prophets hang on these two commandments."

Jesus has now defeated the sharpest minds in the temple. But he does not settle for victory and walk away. Instead, he turns and criticizes the priests in front of the pilgrims. "Everything they do is done for people to see," he tells the crowd. "They love the place of honor at banquets and the most important seats in the synagogues. They love to be greeted in the marketplace and to be called 'Rabbi' by others."

Eventually Jesus departs the temple and will not be seen in public until the time of his arrest. On the way out, he seals his death sentence by predicting the destruction of the temple. "Do you see all these things?" he asks. "Not one stone here will be left on another; every one will be thrown down."

Jesus says these words to his disciples, but a Pharisee overhears. That statement will become a capital crime.

A short time later, as darkness falls, Jesus sits atop the Mount of Olives. A week that began in this very spot with him weeping while astride a donkey now finds him reflective. With the disciples sitting at his side, Jesus speaks in parables so that they will understand the meaning of his words that tell them to live their lives to the fullest. The disciples listen with rapt fascination, but grow concerned as Jesus predicts that after his death, they also will be persecuted and killed. Perhaps to lessen that impact, he shares his thoughts on heaven and promises the disciples that God will reveal himself to them and the world.

Mount of Olives seen from the Bethany Road between 1900 and 1920. [Library of Congress LC-M32-159]

"As you know," Jesus concludes, "the Passover is two days away—and the Son of Man will be handed over to be crucified."

Even as Jesus speaks, the chief priests and the elders are gathered at Caiaphas's palace. They are now in a frenzy. Killing this prophet is the only answer, and time is short. First, Jesus must be arrested. After his arrest, there must be a trial. But the religious laws state that no trials can be held during Passover, and none can be held at night. If they are to kill Jesus, he must be arrested either tomorrow or Thursday and tried before sundown. Making matters even more pressing is the religious stipulation that if a death penalty is ordered, a full night must pass before the sentence can be carried out.

Caiaphas knows that the most important thing right now is to take Jesus into custody. All the other problems can be addressed once that occurs. None of the pilgrims who have thronged to Jesus in the temple courts can be alerted, however, or there could be a riot. A confrontation like that would mean Pontius Pilate would become involved, and Caiaphas will be blamed.

So the arrest must be an act of stealth.

For that, Caiaphas will need some help. Little does he know, but one of Jesus's own disciples is making plans to provide it.

All that traitor wants in return is money.

CHAPTER 21

JUDAS ISCARIOT, BETRAYER

WEDNESDAY, APRIL 4, AD 30 ✦ JERUSALEM ✦ NIGHT

J UDAS ISCARIOT TRAVELS ALONE. JESUS HAS CHOSEN to spend this day in rest, and now he and the other disciples remain behind at the home of Lazarus as Judas walks into Jerusalem. It has been five days since the disciples have arrived in Bethany and three since Jesus rode into Jerusalem on the donkey. Jesus has yet to publicly announce that he is the Christ, nor has he given any indication that he would lead an uprising against Rome. But he has enraged the religious leaders, which has put targets on the back of Jesus and the disciples. "You will be handed over to be persecuted, and put to death, and you will be hated by all the nations because of me," Jesus predicted yesterday when they were all sitting on the Mount of Olives.

Judas did not sign on to be hated or executed. If Jesus can just admit that he is the Christ, then he will triumph over the

Romans. Surely the religious authorities will then be eager to align themselves with him. All this talk of death and execution might come to an end.

So Judas has decided to force Jesus's hand.

The decision was made moments ago during dinner. Mary, sister of Lazarus, approached Jesus to anoint him with perfume. She broke off the thick neck of the flask and poured nard, an exotic scent imported from India, on his head in a show of devotion.

Judas expressed irritation at such a waste of money. Passover, in particular, is a holiday when it is customary to give money to the poor. This time he is not alone in his disgust. Several other disciples join in before Jesus puts an end to the discussion.

"Leave her alone," Jesus orders the disciples. "Why are you bothering her? She has done a beautiful thing to me. The poor you

A page from a 12th-century botanical manuscript.
[Mary Evans Picture Library]

will always have with you, and you can help them any time you want. But you will not always have me. She did what she could. She poured perfume on my body beforehand to prepare for my burial."

Once again, Jesus's words are bewildering. He allows himself to be anointed like the Christ, and yet he is predicting his death.

Judas picks his way carefully down the bumpy dirt road. His journey could be an act of stupidity. He knows that. For he is intent on going directly to the palace of Caiaphas, the most powerful man in the Jewish world. Judas believes that he has an offer of great value that will interest the leader of the Sanhedrin.

Judas is a known disciple of Jesus, however, and this strategy could very well lead to his arrest. And even if nothing like that happens, Judas is uncertain whether an exalted religious leader like Caiaphas will actually meet with an unwashed follower of Jesus.

Making his way from the valley into Jerusalem's gates, Judas navigates through the revelry of the crowded streets to the expensive neighborhoods of the Upper City. He finds the home of Caiaphas and tells the guards his business. Much to his relief, he is warmly welcomed into the spacious palace and led to a lavish room where the high priest is meeting with the other priests and elders.

The conversation immediately turns to Jesus.

"What are you willing to give me if I hand him over to you?" Judas asks.

If the high priests are surprised by Judas's behavior, they don't show it. Their goal is to manipulate Judas into doing whatever it takes to ensure that Jesus is arrested soon and quietly.

"Thirty silver coins," comes the reply.

This is 120 denarii. It is the equivalent of four to six months' wages for a laborer.

Judas has lived the hand-to-mouth existence of Jesus's disciples for two long years, rarely having more than a few extra coins in his purse, and with very little in the way of luxury. And now the chief priest is offering him a lucrative bounty to select a place and time far from the temple courts in which to arrest Jesus.

Judas is a schemer. He has plotted the odds so that they are in his favor and knows that one of two things will happen if he takes the money: Jesus will be arrested and then declare himself to be the Christ. If Jesus truly is the Messiah, then he will have no problem saving himself from Caiaphas and the high priests.

However, if Jesus is not the Christ, then he will die.

Either way, Judas's life will be spared.

Judas and Caiaphas make the deal. The traitorous disciple promises to immediately begin searching for a place to hand over

A denarius coin with the head of Julius Caesar; struck in 44 BC.
[The Bridgeman Art Library]

Jesus. This will mean working closely with the temple guards to arrange the arrest. He will have to slip away from Jesus and the other disciples to alert his new allies of his whereabouts. That may be difficult.

Thirty silver coins are counted out before Judas's eyes. They clang off of one another as they fall into his purse. The traitor is paid in advance.

Judas walks back to Bethany. He wonders how he will explain his absence to Jesus and the others—and where he will hide such a large and noisy bounty.

But it will all work out; he is sure. For Judas truly believes that he is smarter than his compatriots and deserving of reward in this life.

CHAPTER 22

THE LAST SUPPER

THURSDAY, APRIL 5, AD 30 ✦
JERUSALEM ✦ NIGHT

JESUS HAS SO MUCH TO DO IN A VERY SHORT PERIOD of time. He must at last define his life to the disciples. As the final hours before Passover approach, he plans a last meal to share with his followers before saying good-bye, for they have been eyewitnesses to his legacy. And he must trust them to pass it on.

But although those things are vitally important, there is something holding him back—the terrifying prospect of his coming death. Like every citizen of Galilee and Judea, he knows the painful horror and humiliation that await those condemned to die on the cross. Jesus firmly believes he must fulfill what has been written in Scripture, but panic is overtaking him.

So he focuses on his final message to the disciples.

✦   ✦   ✦   ✦   ✦

The entire city of Jerusalem is in an anxious frenzy of last-minute Passover preparation. Everything must be made perfect for the holiday. A lamb must be purchased for the feast—and not just any lamb, but an unblemished one-year-old male. Each home must be cleansed of leavened bread, bread that is made to rise by fermentation, which takes place if ground grain, such as wheat, barley, oats, or rye, is left in water. It is the traditional belief that Moses and the Israelites were forced to flee Egypt without giving their bread a proper time to rise; therefore, leavened products are forbidden on Passover in remembrance of that flight. Everywhere throughout Jerusalem, women sweep floors thoroughly and wipe down counters because even so much as a single crumb can bring forth impurity. At Lazarus's home, Martha and Mary are fastidious in their scrubbing and sweeping. After sundown, Lazarus will walk through the

The inside of the current structure built on the traditional site of the Last Supper, called the Upper Room. [The Bridgeman Art Library]

James Tissot illustration called Women of Galilee.
[The Bridgeman Art Library]

house with an oil lamp in a symbolic search for any traces of leavened products. Finding none—hopefully—he will declare his household ready for Passover.

Even at the palace home of the high priest Caiaphas, slaves and servants search the enormous house for leavened bread. Sinks, ovens, and stoves are scrubbed. Pots and pans are sterilized inside and out by bringing water to a boil, then dropping in a brick to allow the scalding water to overflow. Silverware is heated to a glow, then placed one at a time into boiling water. There is no need, however, to purchase the sacrificial lamb, as Caiaphas's family owns the entire temple lamb concession.

At the former palace of Herod the Great, where Pontius Pilate and his wife, Claudia, once again are enduring Passover, there are no such preparations. The Roman governor begins his day with a shave, for he is clean-shaven and short-haired in the imperial fashion of the day. He cares little for Jewish tradition and does not keep the Jewish customs. For him it is *ientaculum*, *prandium*, and *cena*—breakfast, lunch, and dinner—including plenty of leavened bread. And so the palace is considered unclean. In fact, Caiaphas and the high priests will refrain from entering Herod's palace as the feast draws near, for fear of becoming impure in the presence of the Romans and their pagan ways. This is actually a blessing for Pilate, ensuring him a short holiday from dealing with the Jews and their never-ending problems.

Or so he thinks.

+ + + + +

Judas Iscariot watches Jesus with a quiet intensity, waiting for him to reveal his Passover plans. It would be easy enough to ask the high priest to send temple guards to the home of Lazarus, but arresting Jesus so far from Jerusalem could be a disaster. Too many pilgrims would see him marched back to the city in chains, thus possibly provoking the riot scenario that so terrifies the religious leaders.

Judas is sure that none of the other disciples knows he has betrayed Jesus. So he bides his time, listening and waiting for that moment when Jesus summons his followers and tells them it is time to walk back into Jerusalem. It is hard to believe that Jesus would not return to the holy city at least one more time during their stay. Perhaps Jesus is even waiting for Passover to begin to reveal that he is the Christ. If that is so, then Scripture says this must happen in Jerusalem. Sooner or later, Jesus will go back to the holy city.

+ + + + +

It is evening as Jesus finally leads the disciples back to Jerusalem for their final meal together. A benefactor has kindly rented a room for

Jesus in the Lower City. A long, rectangular table with pillows to rest against is the centerpiece of the room. The space is comfortable, large enough so that conversations can be private but small enough that it will soon sound loud and festive.

Jesus sends John and Peter ahead to find the room and assemble the meal. This is most likely a tense time for Judas Iscariot, for he finally knows that Jesus plans to return to Jerusalem but does not know the hour or the exact location—and even when he obtains this information, he must still find a way to sneak off and alert Caiaphas.

Once in the room, Jesus begins the evening by humbling himself and washing each man's feet with water. This is a task normally reserved for slaves and servants, and certainly not for a venerated teacher of the faith. The disciples are touched by this show of servitude, and the humility it implies. Jesus knows them and their personalities so well, and accepts them without judgment. Their time together has changed the life of every man in this room. And as Jesus carefully and lovingly rinses the road dust from their feet, the depth of his affection is clear.

During dinner, Jesus turns all that good feeling into despair. "Truly I tell you," Jesus says, "one of you will betray me."

The disciples haven't been paying close attention to their leader. The meal has been served and they are reclining, chatting with one another as they pick food from the small plates. But now, shock and sadness fill the room. The disciples each take mental inventory, search for some sign of doubt or weakness that would cause any of them to hand over Jesus. "Surely you don't mean me, Lord?" they ask, one by one. The question goes around the table.

"It is one of the Twelve," Jesus assures them. "One who dips bread into the bowl with me. The Son of Man will go just as it is written about him. But woe to that man who betrays the Son of Man! It would be better for him if he had not been born."

As the conversation roars back to life, with each man wondering to his neighbor about the identity of the betrayer, Peter, in particular, is agitated. He signals to John, who rests on the pillow next to Jesus.

"Ask him which one he means," Peter says.

"Lord, who is it?" John asks. He sits to Jesus's right, while Judas sits on Jesus's immediate left.

"Surely you don't mean me, Rabbi?" Judas blurts out.

"You have said so," Jesus quietly answers. "What you are about to do, do quickly."

The room is noisy as the men talk among themselves, and most miss the final exchange between Judas and Jesus because the two men are sitting so close together. As Judas hastily stands and leaves, some assume that he is off to get more food or drink.

The traitor steps out into the night. Both he and Jesus know exactly where he's going. Jesus once trusted Judas, appointing him treasurer of the disciples, and openly called him friend. But as so often happens when money is involved, years of friendship can quickly evaporate.

Clutching his money bag, Judas walks through the streets and narrow alleys of the Lower City, on up the steep hill to give Caiaphas an outline of Jesus's plans.

CHAPTER 23

JESUS IS ARRESTED

THURSDAY, APRIL 5, AD 30 ✦ GARDEN OF GETHSEMANE ✦ LATE NIGHT

THE HOUR IS LATE. JESUS AND HIS DISCIPLES WALK across the Kidron Valley to an olive garden called Gethsemane at the base of the Mount of Olives. Even though he knows they must be weary from the wine and food, he asks the disciples to stand guard while he climbs the hillside to find a place to be alone.

"Sit here while I pray," he orders the men before ascending the steep slope. "My soul is overwhelmed with sorrow to the point of death," he tells the disciples. "Stay here and keep watch."

The moon is nearly full and provides ample light. Jesus finds a secluded place in the darkness and prays, "Father,

An 1857 photograph of the Garden of Gethsemane looking toward Jerusalem. [The Bridgeman Art Library]

everything is possible for you. Take this cup from me. Yet not what I will, but what you will."

It is a moment of anguish and despair. Jesus knows that he will die. It will be a bloody death on a Roman cross, with all the pain and public ridicule that implies. The people who have been inspired by his words in the temple courts will see him humiliated, and they will not understand how a man who claims to be the Son of God can allow himself to be crucified.

It would be so much easier if Jesus could just escape. He could keep on climbing the hill and walk straight back to Bethany. In the morning, he might journey home to Galilee, there to raise a family and quietly grow old. Jesus does not believe that is his earthly purpose. So he accepts his coming fate and makes no effort to flee.

After about an hour of prayer, Jesus returns to the garden to find the disciples sound asleep. "Couldn't you keep watch for one hour?" he demands.

The disciples don't have an answer. But Jesus once again asks that they stay awake while he returns to his private spot for more prayer.

In the solitude of the night, he asks for the strength to endure all that is to come. "My Father, if it is not possible for this cup to be taken away unless I drink it, may your will be done," Jesus prays.

Jesus walks back down the slope to check on the disciples. All are again asleep, seemingly untroubled by worry or anguish. Jesus walks back up the hill to pray one last time. Finally, he returns to his disciples, exhausted. It is past midnight, the air is growing colder. Jesus wears just his tunic and cloak, which give him little protection from the chill. As he once again enters the garden at Gethsemane, Jesus knows it is time to accept his fate.

"Rise," he tells his disciples, his voice steady. He can clearly see the torches and line of men approaching from across the Kidron Valley. Instead of fleeing, Jesus of Nazareth waits.

✦   ✦   ✦   ✦

The traitor Judas leads a pack of temple guards into the garden. Each man carries either a club or sword, and some also wield the torches and lanterns that cut through the darkness. Yet the flames are not bright enough to ensure that the guards can see which of the bearded men before them is Jesus. Judas has anticipated this and walks casually to Jesus.

"Greetings, Rabbi," he says coldly, kissing Jesus on the cheek. This is the agreed-upon signal between Judas and the temple guards.

Jesus replies, "Do what you came for, friend."

He then turns and looks at the guards. "Who is it you want?"

"Jesus of Nazareth," comes the reply.

"I am he," Jesus answers.

These guards are not Roman soldiers, but Jewish employees of the temple courts. They are physical men, well acquainted with the force needed to make an arrest. Before Jesus's wrists can be tied, however, Peter draws his new sword and cuts off the ear of one of the men.

"Put your sword back in its place," Jesus commands the

ever-impulsive Peter, "for all who draw the sword will die by the sword." Then Jesus submits to be bound and led away.

For Judas, all has gone according to plan. At this late hour, few have seen the commotion.

And so it is that Jesus, his captors, and Judas march across the valley to the palace of Caiaphas, the high priest, on the eve of Passover. Since it is the middle of the night, a trial is not possible. If religious law is to be obeyed, then Jesus must wait until morning to face his accusers. And based on those same laws, if a death sentence is passed the next morning, the mandatory full day of reprieve before execution would mean that Jesus has at least one or two days to live.

Jesus is not counting on the disciples to come to his rescue. Indeed, if he were, that hope would now be futile, for his terrified followers have abandoned him, disappearing into the night.

CHAPTER 24

CAIAPHAS JUDGES JESUS

FRIDAY, APRIL 6, AD 30 ✦ JERUSALEM

INSIDE THE GATES OF JERUSALEM, THE GROUP MARCHES to the Upper City and into the palace of Caiaphas. In the courtyard, Jesus sees not Caiaphas but the high priest's father-in-law, Annas, the aging and regal leader of a priestly dynasty dating back a thousand years. A bleary-eyed Annas stands before Jesus. He is in his mid-fifties, a man whose entire life has revolved around procuring wealth and power. As patriarch, Annas sees that the future of the family dynasty might just rest on how he handles the Jesus situation.

Jesus is asked why he thinks he has been arrested. "I have spoken openly to the world," he says. "I always taught in synagogues or at the temple, where all the Jews come together. I said nothing in secret. Why question me? Ask those who heard me. Surely they know what I said."

Annas and Caiaphas, *painted by James Tissot in
the 19th century.* [The Bridgeman Art Library]

The courtyard is still. Then Jesus is surprised by a sudden and hard blow to the face.

The assault comes out of nowhere, a punch to the head delivered by a short-fused temple guard. "Is this the way you answer the high priest?"

Jesus staggers. The opulent palace room reels. His hands are still bound, and he can neither protect himself nor fight back. But even as Jesus absorbs the blow, he speaks without fear. "If I said something wrong, testify as to what is wrong," Jesus finally tells the guard. "But if I spoke the truth, why did you strike me?"

✦ ✦ ✦ ✦ ✦

As he considers how to handle Jesus, Annas has a great deal at stake. The title of high priest is one that a man carries for life. Rome likes it that way, because it ensures that the money pipeline flows uninterrupted. Annas, his sons, and his son-in-law Caiaphas will all take turns serving as high priest. They will control the sale of temple lambs at Passover, as well as receive a cut of every exchange made by the moneylenders. Outside Jerusalem, the high priests own vast farms and estates. The profits from these ventures, in addition to the taxes extorted from the people of Judea, are all shared with Pilate, and eventually with the Roman emperor Tiberius.

The high priests are far from independent. It is a lesson Annas learned when he was removed from his position by Pontius Pilate's predecessor, Gratus, for imposing and executing death sentences that had been forbidden by the imperial government.

Making the same mistake twice—or allowing Caiaphas to make this mistake—could be catastrophic.

✦ ✦ ✦ ✦ ✦

Everything about Jesus's interrogation is illegal: It takes place at night, Jesus is being asked to incriminate himself without a lawyer, and Annas has no authority to pass sentence. It is also extremely unusual for a prisoner to be brought to the high priest's personal residence, rather than to the prison cells at the Roman barracks.

But Jesus has committed a grave offense—he interrupted the flow of funds from the temple to Rome when he flipped over the money changers' tables. That pipeline is the personal responsibility of Annas. Anyone interfering with the profit-taking must be punished. That, of course, includes Jesus and every single one of his disciples. Annas is determined that he will provide an example of what happens to those who challenge the authority of the temple courts.

Normally, men like Jesus bow to him, pleading for mercy rather than trying to bend his mind with logic at this awful hour, but it is clear that Jesus will not genuflect to any man. And Jesus is capable of great feats of intellect.

Perhaps some time alone with the temple guards will change his attitude. Annas orders a gang of temple guards to escort the prisoner to a quiet place on the palace grounds where they might spend some time together.

Jesus, still bound, is led away. An urgent call goes out through

Jerusalem. The high religious court of the Sanhedrin must assemble immediately.

✦ ✦ ✦ ✦ ✦

Jesus cannot see. The night is dark, and the blindfold covering his eyes shuts out even the minimal light of the small warming fires.

But he can hear extremely well, and the words directed at him are clearly meant to break his spirit. "Prophesy," a temple guard calls out scornfully. Jesus is staggered by another hard punch. "Who hit you?" the guard mocks.

Fists and kicks come from all sides. There is no escape and no respite.

"Who hit you?" the guards call out again and again, landing more blows. "Who hit you?"

The beatings go on for hours, until the temple guards become too tired to continue their savage game.

By the time Jesus is led into Annas's home to confront the Sanhedrin, he is bloodied and bruised. His face is swollen. Exhaustion and weakness caused by loss of blood make it difficult for him to stand, let alone form the coherent arguments that might save him.

Yet once again, the bound and beaten Jesus must rise before his accusers and argue for his life.

The law requires that a person arrested must be taken to the temple courts. But not Jesus. He stands in Annas's family home before as many of the seventy-one members of the Sanhedrin as could be collected. No longer blindfolded, Jesus sees the mosaic floors and the fashionable paintings hanging from the walls.

Despite the late hour, news of Jesus's arrest has made its way around Jerusalem. A small crowd now gathers in the courtyard, warming themselves by the fire pits. A second group stands outside, waiting for any news at the palace's entry gates. Two of the disciples have had second thoughts about abandoning Jesus and have braved arrest to be here. They stand among a number of men loyal to Caiaphas.

Jesus watches as, one by one, Caiaphas's priests are called to testify against him. They stand before the Sanhedrin and brazenly lie about Jesus, spinning fictional stories about what he has said and done. The Sanhedrin listens closely, waiting for the one accusation that might allow them to pass the death sentence.

Throughout the process, Jesus says nothing.

Then comes the accusation for which the Sanhedrin is waiting. "This fellow," swear two men loyal to Caiaphas, "said, 'I am able to destroy the temple of God and rebuild it in three days.'"

Caiaphas has been sitting as he presides over the illegal court. But now he suddenly rises and advances toward Jesus. To his utter fury, Jesus does not contest this allegation.

"Are you not going to answer?" Caiaphas demands with indignation. "What is this testimony that these men are bringing against you?"

Jesus remains silent. He can see the question forming on Caiaphas's lips. It is the query to which everyone in the room wants an answer. Indeed, it is the one question hundreds of thousands here in Jerusalem also want answered. But even as Jesus anticipates what Caiaphas is about to ask next, he also realizes that there is no proper response. His death is imminent, no matter what he says.

"I charge you under oath," fumes Caiaphas, "by the living God: tell us if you are the Messiah, the Son of God."

Silence. Outside, the first birds of morning are stirring and the conversations of passersby can be heard. But in this public room where Caiaphas usually socializes and privately conducts official temple business, none of them utter so much as a syllable as they anxiously await Jesus's decision—will he finally speak?

Jesus *does* answer: "If I tell you, you will not believe me, and if I asked you, you would not answer. But from now on, the Son of Man will be seated at the right hand of the mighty God."

"Are *you* then the Son of God?" the priests demand.

"I am," he tells them.

Then Jesus looks straight at Caiaphas: "And *you* will see the Son of Man sitting at the right hand of the Mighty One and coming on the clouds of heaven."

"He has spoken blasphemy," the high priest tells the Sanhedrin. "Why do we need any more witnesses? Look, now you have heard the blasphemy. What do you think?"

Religious law says that each member of the Sanhedrin must cast a vote when passing sentence. But now there is no vote. The verdict is passed by a simple consensus, although voices of dissent come from Nicodemus and from a wealthy Sadducee named Joseph of Arimathea.

The sun is rising. Jesus has been convicted of blasphemy and sentenced to death. The next step is to convince Pontius Pilate to order his Roman executioners to do the deed.

CHAPTER 25

HEROD JUDGES JESUS

FRIDAY, APRIL 6, AD 30 ✦ JERUSALEM

ACROSS JERUSALEM IN THE ANTONIA FORTRESS, THE dozen men who make up the Roman death squads sit down to *ientaculum*, their big meal of the day. They will most likely not be able to get back to the barracks for the light midday *prandium*, so they enjoy their large portion of porridge. It is often served with cheese and honey to make it even more filling and to provide more energy for the hard labor to come. There is no fruit in season right now, but there is bread, and jugs of weak beer and red wine are spread out on the long communal table.

There are a few condemned men already in the stone dungeons waiting to be crucified. In time, they will be taken into the courtyard for whipping—or *verberatio*, as is it known by

[NEXT PAGES] *Model of the Temple Mount as it may have looked in AD 66. Towers mark the four corners of the Antonia Fortress.* [The Bridgeman Art Library]

the Romans. Low scourging posts are permanently positioned there for this task. Affixed to the top of each post is a metal ring. Each condemned man will be brought out with his hands tied. The executioners will strip him of his clothing and then force him to his knees before binding his hands over his head to the metal ring.

The professional killers now casually eating their morning meal will lash the convicts until they are barely alive. Yet as horrific as the process of lashing might be, it is just the start of the agony. For *verberatio* is a mere prelude to crucifixion.

The soldiers finish their porridge and push back from the table. Time to go to work.

✦ ✦ ✦ ✦ ✦

The condemned Jesus is marched to the palace of Pontius Pilate. The sound of his sandals, and those of Caiaphas, other high priests of the Sanhedrin, and temple guards who surround him, echo off the cobblestones. It is still early morning, and Jerusalem is just waking up.

Caiaphas demands an immediate audience with Pilate. But since the high priest cannot enter a Gentile residence so close to Passover, he requests that Pilate come down to the gate. It is a gross violation of their formal relationship, but Caiaphas hopes Pilate will understand.

It takes a while to get word to Pilate and for the prefect to dress and make his way to the gate. He cannot be pleased to be faced with the sight of temple guards, lavishly dressed priests, and a prisoner clearly in an advanced state of physical suffering.

"What charges are you bringing against this man?" Pilate asks gruffly.

Caiaphas has been dreading this moment. For while he wants the Romans to kill Jesus, the charge of blasphemy is a Jewish offense. Rome could not care less about it. And Pilate, with his intolerance

Roman soldiers with shields and spear. Hand-colored German print; no date. [North Wind Picture Library]

for the Jews, is not the sort to risk his career by allowing Jewish law to dictate whom he executes.

"If he were not a criminal, we would not have handed him over to you," Caiaphas replies, avoiding the question.

Pilate is not easily swayed. "Take him yourselves and judge him by your own law."

"But we have no right to execute anyone," Caiaphas responds.

"I find no basis for a charge against this man," Pilate replies.

Another of the priests speaks up. "He stirs up the people all over Judea by his teaching. He started in Galilee and has come all the way here."

"He's a Galilean?" Pilate demands. In this simple question, he sees a way out of this mess. The Sanhedrin is clearly luring him into a political trap. But if Jesus is a Galilean, this matter is better suited for Herod Antipas. Galilee is the tetrarch's jurisdiction, and Antipas is staying in a palace just a few blocks away.

Pilate refuses to accept custody of Jesus. He dismisses the entire gathering and orders the prisoner to be bound over to Antipas. Once again, Jesus is marched through the early dawn streets of upper Jerusalem. There is no sign of the peasant pilgrims from Galilee or any of the other poorer class of Jews, for they have no reason to be wandering through this wealthy neighborhood at such an early hour. Slaves can be seen sweeping the porches of the masters' homes, while inside the wealthy take their morning meal.

But if Pilate thinks he has escaped from Caiaphas's snare, he is wrong. For soon the entire temple group, including Jesus, returns.

Herod Antipas was most delighted to finally meet Jesus and spent a short time evaluating him. The tetrarch even requested a miracle for his own personal amusement.

Antipas has no fear of Caiaphas or the high priests, for they have no power over him. So even as they launched volley after volley of accusation against Jesus, hoping to swing the tetrarch over to their side, Antipas refused to listen. Getting pulled into a power struggle between the temple and Rome would be most unwise. Besides, he is haunted by the death of John the Baptist. The last thing Antipas wants is the blood of another preacher on his hands.

Even though Jesus refused to perform a miracle, Antipas sees no reason to condemn him to death. He let his soldiers have their fun, allowing them to taunt Jesus and ridicule him by questioning his royalty before placing an old military mantle on the prisoner's shoulders. It is purple, the color of kings.

CHAPTER 26

PILATE JUDGES JESUS

FRIDAY, APRIL 6, AD 30 ✦ JERUSALEM

Now, once again, Pilate stands at his palace gates, debating what to do about Jesus. He is running out of options. Clearly, he cannot order the Jews to release the man, for that would be interfering in their religious law—and Emperor Tiberius has made it quite clear that Roman governors cannot do this.

Still, he doesn't have to accept the prisoner. He could order that Jesus be sent over to the Antonia Fortress, there to be held until after Passover—perhaps long after Passover, when Pilate has already left town. Above all, Pontius Pilate does not want trouble. So he finally sends Caiaphas on his way and reluctantly accepts custody of Jesus.

The fate of Jesus is now in the hands of Rome.

✦ ✦ ✦ ✦ ✦

Pontius Pilate is curious. "Are you the king of the Jews?" he asks Jesus. The governor is seated on a throne of judgment, looking down upon an open-air courtyard paved with flagstones. A small audience watches.

Pilate has chosen this location for many reasons. It is near where his small personal garrison is housed. This courtyard is not actually in the palace, but adjacent to it. Its unique architecture allows Pilate to address his subjects from an elevated position, while also providing him a private door to the palace and through which prisoners like Jesus can be led out and tried, then quietly walked back to the prison cells.

Another advantage to the location is that since it's not actually inside the residence, Jews are permitted to enter on the eve of Passover. Temple priests and Caiaphas's disciples are present, carefully monitoring the proceedings for their leader. They are there to ensure that the sentence passed by Caiaphas and the Sanhedrin is carried out.

"Is that your own idea, or did others talk to you about me?" Jesus asks in return.

"Am I a Jew?" Pilate asks. "It was your own people and chief priests handed you over to me. What is it you have done?"

"My kingdom is not of this world. If it were, my servants would fight to prevent my arrest. But my kingdom is from another place."

"You are a king, then!" says an amused Pilate. This is good news for the governor, for by declaring himself to be sovereign, Jesus has now committed a crime against Rome and the emperor. He is now a serious threat to public order. Whatever happens next can be justified.

"You say that I am a king. In fact, the reason I was born and came into the world is to testify to the truth. Everyone on the side of the truth listens to me," Jesus responds.

"What is truth?" Pilate asks, now fascinated by Jesus.

But if the Roman was expecting an answer to that question, he is disappointed, as Jesus stands mute.

Pilate turns his attention from Jesus to the disciples of the Jewish temple who fill the courtyard. From his lofty perch, he can look down upon the group, measuring their reaction.

It is customary for the Roman prefect to release a prisoner at the time of the Passover. Now Pilate finds a simple solution that might ease him out of this politically volatile situation: he will give the crowd a choice between releasing the peaceful Jesus or the horrific Barabbas, a well-known terrorist and murderer whose crimes truly deserve punishment.

"Do you want me to release the king of the Jews?" Pilate asks the crowd.

The response surprises him. For Pilate is not aware that the people he is speaking to have been ordered by the high priests and religious elders to make sure that Jesus is executed. It is not the Jewish pilgrims who want Jesus dead, nor most of the residents of Jerusalem. No, it is a small handful of men who enrich themselves through the temple. To them, a man who speaks the truth is far more dangerous than a mass murderer.

"Give us Barabbas," they shout back.

CHAPTER 27

LASHED

FRIDAY, APRIL 6, AD 30 ✦ JERUSALEM

WHILE JESUS IS BEING JUDGED, THE BUSINESS OF Passover begins in the temple courts. Despite their sleepless night, Caiaphas and the other priests cannot afford the luxury of a morning's rest. Soon they walk across the bridge connecting the Upper City with the temple and prepare to go about their day. Already, long lines of pilgrims are forming, and the incessant bleating of lambs fills the air.

The first sacrifices will take place at noon, in keeping with the law. Rows of priests are now assembling, some carrying silver bowls, and others gold. These are for catching the blood of the lamb as its throat is slit. The bowls are then carried to the altar, and the blood poured in sacrifice. A choir is gathering as well, along with men who will honor this great day with blasts from their silver trumpets.

✦ ✦ ✦ ✦ ✦

Pontius Pilate does not care about what is happening inside the temple. The focus of his attention is the problem still standing before him. The Roman governor does not believe that executing such a popular figure as Jesus is a wise decision. Any unrest among the people following an execution of this sort will certainly be reported to Emperor Tiberius, and any fallout laid at Pilate's feet.

So rather than crucify Jesus, Pilate sentences him to lashing. He hopes that will appease the Sanhedrin. The Roman governor calls the high priests and church elders together to announce this decision. "You brought me this man as one who was inciting the people to rebellion. I have examined him in your presence and found no basis for your charges against him. Neither has Herod, for he sent him back to us; as you can see, he has done nothing to deserve death. Therefore, I will punish him and release him."

Within moments, Jesus is stripped and led to the scourging pole.

Jesus endures. As with any other victim, his hands are manacled to the metal ring atop the post, rendering him unable to move. Two legionnaires with whips stand behind him, one on either side. A third stands to one side. He holds an abacus, so that he might keep track of the numbers of blows that will be inflicted. The fourth member of the death squad stands by to replace any member who tires in his duties. Watching over all of them is the *exactor mortis*, the supervisor.

Jesus feels the lash. There is no pause between the blows. The instant one executioner pulls back his whip, the other unfurls his lash across Jesus's back. Even when the tendrils of leather and lead get tangled, the soldiers don't stop. The most lashes a man can receive under the laws of Moses are "forty minus one," but the Romans don't always pay attention to Jewish legalities. Pilate has told these men to lash Jesus, and now they do so until he is physically broken but not yet dead.

That is the order. Scourge him, but under no circumstances is he to be killed.

After the whipping, Jesus is unchained and helped to his feet. He has cried out in pain during his scourging, and he is losing a great deal of blood. The lash marks extend down to the backs of his calves. He is in the early stages of shock.

The Roman death squad has clearly done its job. Striking at Jesus with surgical precision, they have beaten him almost to death. Pilate has made it clear that this will be the extent of their duties today. Yet they stand by for more, just in case.

Jesus's hands are still tied in front of him. He is slowly led back to the prison, where the Roman soldiers have their own brand of fun with this unique prisoner. Jesus does nothing as they drape that filthy purple cloak over his body, knowing it will soon stick to his wounds. The soldiers then make a pretend ruler's scepter, or wand, from a reed and thrust it into Jesus's hands, again mocking his claim to be king. Rather than take pity on a man who has just endured a scourging, the soldiers spit on him.

Not content to leave the suffering man alone, the soldiers guarding Jesus now up the ante. In an atrocious display, they begin to cut pieces from a tall white shrub with rigid elliptical leaves, small green flowers, and inch-long curving thorns that grow closely together. The soldiers are more than willing to endure the prick of these

Jesus is led to Pontius Pilate. Bronze panel from the doors to Basilica Parrocchiale Santa Maria del Popolo in Rome, Italy. [Alamy]

sharp spikes as they weave several branches together to form a crown. When they are done, this wreath makes a perfect complement to the scepter and purple cloak. All hail the king.

Jesus is too weak to protest when the crown of thorns is fitted onto his head and the spikes pressed hard into his skin. Blood pours down his face. Jesus stands humiliated in the small prison as soldiers dance around him—some punching him, others spitting, and still others getting down on both knees to praise their "king."

But just when it seems that Jesus can't take any more, the soldiers receive word that Pilate would like to see the prisoner. Once again, he is led out into the public square, where the Sanhedrin and its loyal followers stand waiting.

Jesus's vision has blurred. Fluid is slowly building around his lungs. He is having a hard time breathing. He has predicted his death all along, but the details of his demise are shocking.

The high priests and religious leaders watch as Jesus steps forth, the crown of thorns still on his head. They remember that Jesus humiliated them in the temple courts just three days ago. They can see his suffering now. Yet they have no sympathy. Jesus must die, the more painfully, the better.

It is mid-morning as Pilate takes his seat again on the judgment throne. He tries one last time to release Jesus. "Here is your king," he snarls at the assembly of religious leaders and their disciples. These men should be in the temple courts, for the slaughter of the lambs is soon to begin.

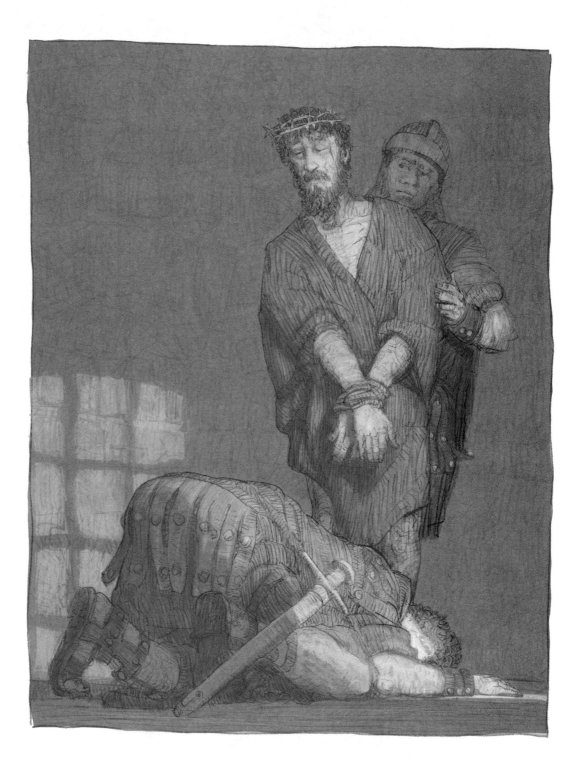

"Take him away," the religious leaders chant. "Take him away. Crucify him."

Pilate is tired of arguing. The Roman governor is not known for his compassion and believes he has done all that he can do. The fate of Jesus is simply not worth the effort.

"Shall I crucify your king?" he asks, seeking a final confirmation.

"We have no king but Caesar," a chief priest replies. If taken at face value, those words are an act of heresy, for he has rejected his own Jewish God in favor of a god of the Roman pagans. Yet the followers of the Sanhedrin see no irony in the situation.

"What crime has he committed?" Pilate yells back.

"Crucify him!" comes the response.

Pilate orders that a small bowl of water be brought to him. He dips his hands into the chalice and theatrically makes a show of ritual cleansing. "I am innocent of this man's blood," he tells the religious leaders. "It is your responsibility."

But in fact, the responsibility belongs to Pilate. Only the Roman governor possesses the *ius gladii*—the right of the sword. Or, as it is also known, the right to execute.

So it is that Pilate orders his executioners to take control of Jesus. As they lead him away to be crucified, Pontius Pilate prepares for an early lunch.

CHAPTER 28

CRUCIFIED

**FRIDAY, APRIL 6, AD 30 ✦ GOLGOTHA ✦
MID-MORNING TO AFTERNOON**

T HE PURPLE CLOAK IS RIPPED AWAY, BUT THE CROWN of thorns remains. The death squad places a chunk of unfinished wood on Jesus's shoulders. It weighs between fifty and seventy pounds and is just a little less than six feet long. Its splinters quickly find their way into his open wounds.

The humiliation at Pilate's palace now complete, the procession toward the place of execution begins.

At the front of the line is the *exactor mortis*. By tradition, this centurion holds up a sign written in Greek, Aramaic, and Latin. Today, the words JESUS THE NAZARENE: KING OF THE JEWS are written on the sign. Normally, a man's crimes are listed on the sign, which will be nailed onto the cross above him. This way, any passerby will know why the man was crucified. So if treason is the charge, then that is what the sign should state.

But Pontius Pilate is changing tradition. In a last attempt to get the better of Caiaphas, the governor writes the inscription himself.

"Change it," Caiaphas demands before the crucifixion procession gets under way.

Pilate refuses, his condescension apparent.

So the sign leads the way as Jesus and his four executioners make the painfully slow journey to Golgotha, the hill used as the Roman execution ground. The trip is slightly less than half a mile, taking Jesus through the cobbled streets of Jerusalem's Upper City, then out the Gennath Gate to the low hill on which a vertical pole awaits his arrival. It is getting close to noon. A substantial crowd has gathered to watch, despite a blazing sun overhead.

The *exactor mortis* becomes concerned as Jesus repeatedly stumbles. As a former builder and carpenter, Jesus knows the proper way to carry a length of lumber but now lacks the strength to do so. He is constantly on the verge of fainting. Should Jesus die before reaching the place of execution, it is the *exactor mortis* who will be held responsible. So a pilgrim bystander, an African Jew named Simon of Cyrene, is enlisted to carry the crossbar for Jesus.

The procession continues.

Meanwhile, just a few hundred yards away in the temple courts, the celebration of Passover is in progress, diverting the attention of many who revere Jesus and who might riot to intervene and save his life.

The execution site, Golgotha, is not a large hill. It is a low rise close to Jerusalem's city wall. As the procession arrives atop

Golgotha, the soldiers send Simon away and hurl the crossbar onto the dirt. The death squad takes control. They force Jesus to the ground, laying his torso atop the upper crossbeam, known as the *patibulum*. His hands are then stretched out, and two soldiers put all their weight on his extended arms, even as another approaches with a thick mallet and an iron nail with a square shaft. This spike is six inches long.

The soldier hammers the sharpened point into Jesus's wrist. Jesus cries out in pain as the iron pierces its mark. The Romans use the wrist location because the nail never hits bone and passes all the way through to the wood in just a few sharp swings of the hammer. The wrist bones, mean-while, surround the soft tis-sue, forming a barrier. So when the cross is hoisted upward, and Jesus's body weight is suspended from those spikes, the bones keep the thin layer of muscle from ripping and prevent him from fall-ing to the ground.

The first wrist secure, the executioner moves on to the second. A crowd watches from the base of the hill. Among them are Jesus's devoted friend Mary Magdalene and his mother, Mary. She came to Jerusalem for Passover, not having any idea what would befall her son. Now Mary can do nothing but look on in anguish.

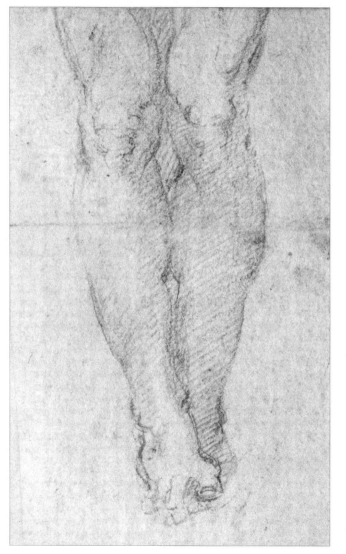

After Jesus is nailed to the crossbar, the executioners hoist him to his feet. A careful balancing act ensues, because the weight of the wood is now on Jesus's back—not his shoulders. In his weakened state, he could easily fall over. Two soldiers hold up the ends of the crossbar, while a third steadies Jesus as they back him toward the vertical beam that will complete the cross.

The *staticulum*, as this in-ground pole is known, is close to eight feet tall. One

Study for a crucifixion by Michelangelo. Black chalk on paper.
[The Bridgeman Art Library]

soldier grabs Jesus around the waist and lifts him up as the other two hoist their ends of the crossbar. The fourth executioner stands atop a ladder that leans against the *staticulum*, guiding the crossbar into the small joint that has been carved into the top of the vertical piece. The weight of Jesus's body holds the beam inside the groove.

And so it is that Jesus of Nazareth now hangs on the cross. Another moment of agony comes when his knees are bent slightly and then the feet lapped one over the other and nailed into place.

Finally, in the spot directly over Jesus's head, the sign carried by the *executor mortis* is nailed to the cross. Their physical work done, the death squad begins mocking Jesus, throwing dice for his once-fine tunic and calling up to him, "If you are the king of the Jews, save yourself." The Roman death squad will remain on Golgotha until Jesus dies. They will drink their sour wine and even offer some to Jesus.

Three hours pass. The Passover celebration continues inside the temple courts, and the sounds of singing and blowing trumpets resound across the city to the execution site. Indeed, Jesus can see the Temple Mount quite clearly from his place on the cross. He knows that many are still waiting for him. The news of his execution has not traveled far, much to the delight of Pilate and Caiaphas, who still fear the possibility of Jesus's supporters starting a riot when they hear of his murder.

"I am thirsty," Jesus finally says. His voice is not more than a whisper. A soldier soaks a sponge in sour wine and reaches up to place it to Jesus's lips, knowing that the liquid will sting. Jesus sucks in the tart fluid. Shortly afterward, he gazes on Jerusalem one last time before the inevitable happens.

"It is finished," he says.

Jesus bows his head. He lapses into unconsciousness. His neck relaxes. His entire body rolls forward, pulling his neck and shoulders away from the cross. Only the nails in his hands hold him in place.

The man who once preached so fearlessly, who walked far and wide to give his people hope, and whose message of love reached thousands during his lifetime—and will one day reach billions more—stops breathing.

Jesus of Nazareth is dead. He is thirty-six years old.

CHAPTER 29

ENTOMBED

APRIL 6, AD 30 ✦ GOLGOTHA ✦ LATE AFTERNOON

T HE RACE IS ON. THE ROMAN DEATH SQUAD HAS HAD A hard day, but there is still more work to be done. It is their usual practice to leave a man on the cross for days after he dies. But Jewish law dictates that a body cannot remain on a "tree" during the Sabbath, which begins at sundown today and continues throughout Saturday. So the men must take Jesus down from the cross. First, the *executor mortis* verifies Jesus's death by thrusting a spear into his chest. Body fluid pours out, mixed with blood. Extracting the spear tip, the captain of the guard then orders his men to remove Jesus from the cross. It is a crucifixion in reverse, with the men using ladders and teamwork to bring Jesus and the crossbar back to the ground. Once again, Jesus is laid flat. But now the death squad works hard to remove the nails—unbent. Iron is expensive, and spikes are reused as much as possible.

Most who witnessed Jesus's crucifixion have departed. Mary, his mother, and Mary Magdalene are among those who remain. But as the soldiers now go about the hard physical labor of uncrucifying a man, the Sadducee named Joseph of Arimathea steps forward. This wealthy member of the Sanhedrin and secret disciple of Jesus was one of the few dissenting voices during the illegal trial. Another of those voices was that of Nicodemus the Pharisee, and he, too, is present. They have received permission from Pilate to take the body, as the governor wants to put this execution to rest as soon as possible.

Somewhat shockingly, Joseph and Nicodemus are publicly declaring their allegiance to Jesus. Joseph takes Jesus to his own private family tomb, a brand-new man-made cave carved out of the soft Jerusalem rock on a nearby hillside. The Jews believe that to touch a dead body on Passover makes one unclean and disqualifies the person from eating the Seder meal. By law, Joseph and Nicodemus will be declared impure and must undergo a seven-day cleansing ritual.

No matter, these two bold men express their discipleship as followers of Jesus by carrying his limp corpse down from Golgotha and then to the nearby tomb, where they lay it down on the carved rock ledge. There is no time to perform the ritual washing and anointing of the corpse with oil. But they do make the gesture of

Wood carving of the entombment of Jesus carved in the 16th century, from the Beguine Convent in Cambrai, France. [The Bridgeman Art Library]

coating the body in expensive myrrh and aloes, to overwhelm the coming smell of decomposition. Then they wrap the body tightly in linen, making sure to keep it loose around Jesus's face in case he is not really dead, but merely unconscious. In this way, he will not suffocate. Jewish tradition dictates that all bodies be examined three days after apparent death. Thus, the tomb will be reopened, and Jesus will be observed on Sunday.

But all of this is merely adherence to ritual. For Jesus is clearly dead.

The men say a formal good-bye and then step outside the tomb. A hand-carved round stone weighing hundreds of pounds is in position at the top of a downhill slope. Mary, the mother of Jesus, watches as the two men strain to roll the stone across the tomb entrance. The shaft of daylight penetrating the tomb grows smaller and smaller as the rock rolls into position.

When death is formally pronounced on Sunday, Jesus's body will rest inside the tomb for a full year. Then his bones will be removed and placed in a small stone jar known as an ossuary, either to be stored in a niche carved into the tomb wall or removed to a new location.

Jesus of Nazareth predicted his death. Now it is done, and the silence of the grave is complete. Alone in the darkness of the tomb, Jesus of Nazareth finally rests in peace.

The Shroud of Turin, a centuries-old linen cloth that bears the image of a crucified man. Some believe it is the cloth used to wrap Jesus in the tomb. [Corbis]

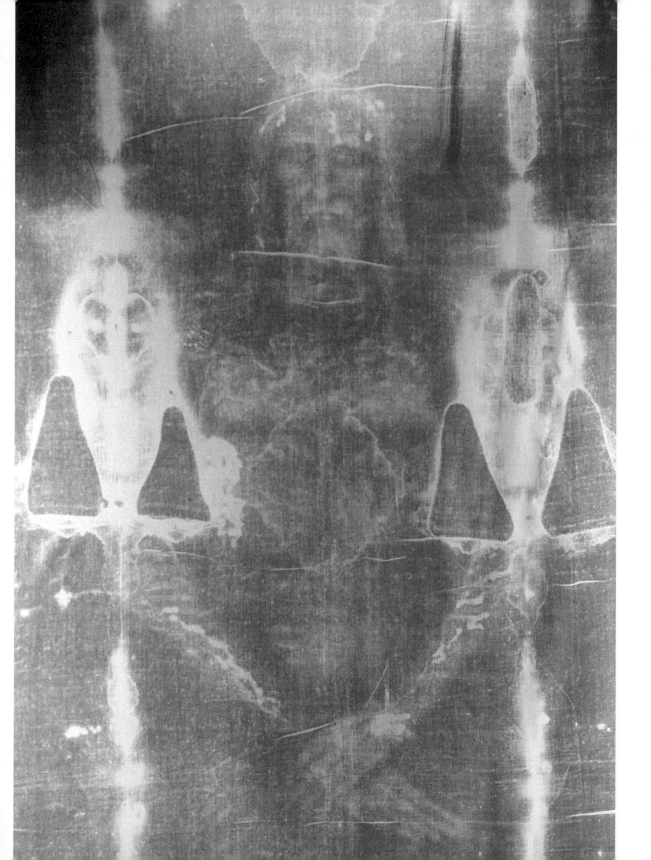

CHAPTER 30

GUARDED

SATURDAY, APRIL 7, AD 30 ✦ PILATE'S PALACE, JERUSALEM ✦ DAY

PONTIUS PILATE HAS VISITORS. ONCE AGAIN, CAIAPHAS and the Pharisees stand before him. But now they are inside the palace, no longer fearful of being made unclean by the governor's presence, for Passover is done.

For the first time, Pilate notices that Caiaphas is actually terrified of Jesus's power. What was not so obvious in Jesus's lifetime is now quite apparent in death, for the chief priest is making an unheard-of request. Caiaphas tells Pilate directly, "That deceiver said, 'After three days I will rise again.' So give the order for the tomb to be made secure until the third day. Otherwise, his disciples may come and steal the body and tell the people that he has been raised from the dead."

There is a certain logic to the request, for the disappearance of Jesus's body might lead to an uprising if his followers convinced people that this man who claimed to be the Christ had actually proven himself to be immortal.

Pilate consents.

"Take a guard," he orders. "Go, make the tomb as secure as you know how."

And so it is that a guard is placed at the tomb of Jesus, just in case the dead man tries to escape.

For Rome and the temple, that should have been the end of it. The troublemaker and blasphemer is dead. If Jesus's followers have any plan for trouble, there is no sign of it. The disciples have proven themselves timid, still stunned that their Messiah is dead. They have gone into hiding and pose no threat to Rome.

Pilate is relieved. Soon he will be on his way back to Caesarea, there to once again govern without the constant interference of the temple priests.

But Caiaphas will not go away. Wearing his expensive robes and linen, he postures before Pilate, not knowing what the Roman governor will report back to Rome. Caiaphas has much at stake, and he is uneasy over Pilate's hand-washing display. He will lose everything if Emperor Tiberius blames him for the death of Jesus. And so Caiaphas stands firm, looking for any sign of approval from Pilate. But the Roman governor has had enough of this arrogant priest. Without a word, he stands and walks away.

CHAPTER 31

THE TOMB IS EMPTY

SUNDAY, APRIL 8, AD 30 ✦
JESUS'S TOMB ✦ DAWN

T HE MORNING IS DARK. DAWN WILL SOON BREAK OVER
Jerusalem, marking the third day since Jesus's death. Mary
Magdalene now takes it upon herself to perform the traditional task of examining the dead body. She travels with another
woman named Mary—though not the mother of Jesus. Just as
on the day Jesus was executed, the streets of the Upper City are
quiet as the two women pass through. They exit the city walls
at the Gennath Gate and now travel in Jesus's footsteps as they
walk toward Golgotha.

The vertical pole on which Jesus was crucified still stands
on the hill, awaiting the next crucifixion. The two Marys look
away from the gruesome object and walk around the hill to
Jesus's tomb.

They have practical matters on their minds. Mary Magdalene has not forgotten the many kindnesses Jesus showed her

during his lifetime. And just as she once anointed him with perfume and washed his feet with her tears, so now she plans to anoint the body with spices. It is unconscionable to her that Jesus's corpse molders and emits a foul smell. Perhaps a year from now, when she returns for Passover and is among those who roll away the stone in front of Jesus's tomb to collect his bones, the smell of sweet perfume will pour forth from the cave entrance instead of the stench of death.

But this presents another immediate challenge: Mary is physically incapable of rolling away the tombstone. She will require help, but most of Jesus's disciples are still in hiding.

As the two Marys approach the tomb, they are stunned. The tombstone has been rolled away. The cave is empty. No one is standing guard.

Mary Magdalene cautiously steps forward and looks inside. She smells the myrrh and aloes with which Jesus was anointed. She sees the linen shroud that wrapped the body. But there is nothing else there.

To this day, the body of Jesus of Nazareth has never been found.

AFTERWORD

WHAT COMES NEXT IS THE VERY ROOT OF THE CHRISTIAN faith. The New Testament gospels that most believe were written by the disciples Matthew, Mark, Luke, and John many years after Jesus's death record that Jesus's body was not stolen. Instead, this Scripture says that Jesus rose from the dead and ascended into heaven. After his body was discovered to be missing, the gospels state that Jesus appeared twelve times on Earth over a forty-day period. Witnesses to these apparitions range from a single individual to groups of more than five hundred on a mountain in Galilee. Some in that large crowd spoke vividly of the event for years to come. Twenty-five years later, the disciple Paul included the mountain appearance in a letter he wrote to an early Christian group in Corinth, Greece. The belief in the divinity of Jesus is at the core of the Christian faith.

The Jews of today do not believe that Jesus was the Messiah, but consider him simply a man, because he did not fulfill the prophecy that the anointed one would build a Third Temple, gather all Jews back to Israel, and usher in an era of world peace.

Buddhists believe that Jesus was an enlightened man whose teachings were similar to those of the Buddha.

To Hindus, Jesus was an incarnation of God, a saint, and a wise teacher.

Muslims believe that Jesus was one of many true prophets sent by God but superseded by Muhammad.

Whether or not one believes that Jesus rose from the dead, the story of his life and the message he preached achieved much greater status after his crucifixion. Unlike other preachers and prophets, such as Judas of Gamala, Jesus became a noted personage in the history of Jerusalem and beyond.

✦ ✦ ✦ ✦ ✦

After the crucifixion, the disciples of Jesus underwent a radical shift in behavior. They were quite positive that they had seen a resurrected Jesus and soon went out into the world and fearlessly preached his message. Known as the apostles, ones who are sent out to teach, all but one of the men paid a tremendous price for their faith.

In AD 44, the grandson of Herod the Great, Herod Agrippa, who ruled Judea at that time, ordered that **JAMES** be put to the sword. The beheading of James made him the first disciple to be martyred. Agrippa was violently opposed to Christianity and used his power to ruthlessly suppress the followers of Jesus.

For a time Agrippa imprisoned **PETER,** but did not kill him. Peter's missionary work eventually took him to Rome, where he formalized the new Catholic Church. The Romans reacted by sentencing Peter to death on the cross. The year is thought to be sometime around AD 64. There is good evidence that Peter is buried beneath St. Peter's Cathedral in Vatican City.

The deaths of most disciples are more legend than fact. **ANDREW**, the apostle known for being optimistic and enterprising, preached Jesus's message in what is now the Ukraine, Russia,

and Greece. He is believed to have been crucified in Patras, a Roman-controlled region of Greece.

The often-pessimistic **THOMAS** is thought to have been speared to death near Madras, in India. **BARTHOLOMEW** preached in Egypt, Arabia, and what is now Iran before being flayed—skinned alive—then beheaded in India. **SIMON THE ZEALOT** is thought to have been sawed in half for his preaching in Persia. **PHILIP** preached in what is now western Turkey. He is said to have been martyred by having hooks run through his ankles and then being hung upside down in the Greco-Roman city of Hieropolis. The gregarious former tax collector **MATTHEW** may have died in Ethiopia, murdered like all the rest for his fervent preaching.

Little is known about what happened to the others, except that each disciple spent his life preaching and all but one was killed for doing so. It is a fact that the disciples of Jesus traveled as far as Africa, India, and Britain in their zeal to spread their faith, marking a sea change from their timid behavior during Jesus's life and in the hours after his death.

The last to die was **JOHN**, who was taken prisoner by the Romans for preaching Christianity and exiled to the Greek island of Patmos. There he wrote his gospel and also what would become the final pages of the Christian New Testament, the Book of Revelation. John died in AD 100 in Ephesus, in what is now Turkey. He was ninety-four, and the only apostle not to have been martyred.

Matthew's gospel and the First Book of Acts attribute **JUDAS ISCARIOT**'s death to suicide. Matthew writes that upon learning that his plan to force Jesus's hand had resulted in the execution order, Judas flung his thirty pieces of silver into the temple and hanged himself from a tree. Legend has it that he used a horse's halter to break his own neck. Whether or not this is true, Judas Iscariot was never heard from again.

The same is true for **MARY MAGADALENE.** After her appearance at the tomb of Jesus, she disappears from the story.

MARY, THE MOTHER OF JESUS, is mentioned in the Book of Acts and alluded to in the Book of Revelation as "a woman clothed with the sun," but her fate goes unrecorded. On November 1, 1950, the Roman Catholic Church decreed that her body had been "assumed into heaven." Pope Pius XII noted that Mary, "having completed the course of her earthly life, was assumed body and soul into heavenly glory."

✦ ✦ ✦ ✦ ✦

Six years after washing his hands of Jesus's execution, **PONTIUS PILATE** intervened in another case involving a preacher—and this time it cost him his job. The man from Samaria had holed up in a mountaintop sanctuary in Gerizim. Concerned by the man's growing legion of followers, Pilate suppressed the movement with heavily armed Roman soldiers. This resulted in many deaths, and led Pilate to be recalled to Rome to explain his actions. He thought his appeal would be heard by his friend, **EMPEROR TIBERIUS**. But by the time Pilate reached Rome, Tiberius was dead. The fourth-century historian Eusebius

The ossuary of the high priest Caiaphas, the chest his remains were put in after time in a tomb. [The Bridgeman Art Library]

records that Pilate was forced to commit suicide, becoming "his own murderer and executioner." Where and how Pilate died is still debated. One report says he drowned himself in the Rhone River near Vienne, a city in modern-day France. There a Roman monument still stands in the heart of the city and is often referred to as "Pilate's Tomb." Another report says he hurled himself into a lake near what is now Lausanne, Switzerland, where Mount Pilatus is said to have been named in his honor. There is also a rumor that Pilate and his wife, Claudia, converted to Christianity and were killed for their faith.

With Pilate gone, **Caiaphas** was left without a Roman political ally. He had many enemies in Jerusalem and was soon replaced as the temple high priest. Caiaphas then left the stage and disappeared from history. The dates of his birth and death are unrecorded. But in 1990 an ossuary believed to contain his bones was discovered in Jerusalem. They are currently on display at the Israel Museum.

Herod Antipas may have been well

schooled in palace intrigue, but it eventually brought about his demise. His nephew Agrippa was known to be a close friend of the Roman emperor Caligula. The Jewish historian Josephus relates that when Antipas foolishly asked Caligula to name him king, instead of tetrarch (at the suggestion of his wife, **HERODIAS,** who continued to get him into trouble), it was Agrippa who lodged charges that Antipas was plotting to assassinate Caligula. As proof, Agrippa pointed to the enormous arsenal of weaponry possessed by Antipas's army. So it was that Caligula ordered Antipas to spend the rest of his life exiled in Gaul (now France). His fortune and territories were handed over to the younger Agrippa. The former tetrarch was joined by his wife. The two lived in Lugdunum, which many believe to be the location of modern-day Lyon.

THE HISTORY AFTER JESUS'S DEATH

THE TENSION BETWEEN ROME AND THE JEWISH PEOPLE DID not lessen after the murder of Jesus. In AD 66, the Jews waged war on the Roman occupying army and took control of Jerusalem. However, the Romans did not accept defeat.

By AD 70, they had surrounded the city with four Roman legions and were laying siege. Pilgrims arriving to celebrate Passover were allowed into the city—then not allowed to leave, putting considerable pressure on Jerusalem's limited water and food supplies. Those attempting to escape were promptly crucified and their crosses left on the surrounding hills to warn Jewish residents of the fate that awaited them. Thousands were eventually nailed to the cross during the siege, so many that the Romans ran out of wood. Trees had to be logged and carried to Jerusalem from miles away in order to accommodate the tremendous number of crucifixions.

When the Romans finally breached the city walls, the destruction was total. Those Jews who didn't escape were killed or enslaved. The temple itself was burned to the ground and much of the city leveled.

Four hundred years later, in AD 476, the Roman Empire was toppled by Germanic tribes. However, long before the empire's collapse, Rome turned away from its pagan gods and began worshipping Jesus Christ. Christianity was officially legalized throughout the Roman Empire in 313.

[FOLLOWING PAGES] *The destruction of the temple in AD 70; 19th-century painting by Francesco Hayez.* [The Bridgeman Art Library]

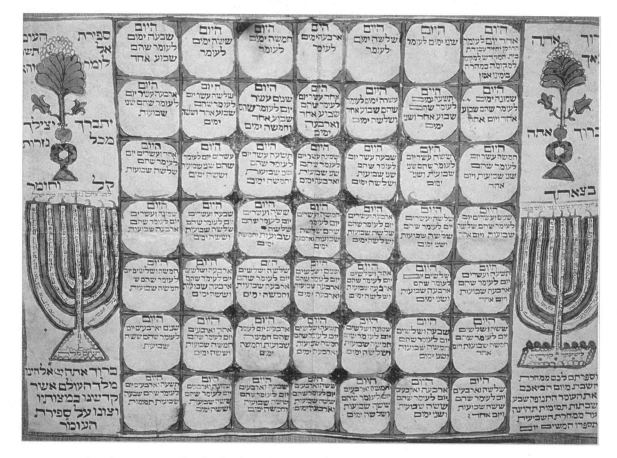

A 19th-century Jewish calendar from the Israel Museum in Jerusalem. [Mary Evans Picture Library]

COUNTING YEARS

WE USE CALENDARS TO FIX CERTAIN LENGTHS OF TIME—days, months, and years—and to measure the passage of these lengths of time. The calendar we use today was devised in the sixth century and approved by the Roman Catholic pope Gregory XIII. His calendar makers used the presumed birth of Jesus, in AD 1, as the dividing point. The years before AD 1 are often labeled as BC, meaning "Before Christ." AD stands for *Anno Domini*, the Latin for "the Year of Our Lord." (Today, many historians prefer not to use a religious-based calendar notation and use BCE and CE, meaning Before the Common Era and Common Era, respectively.)

Jewish people have a calendar that counts time from the year before the estimated creation of the world. This calendar is used to determine the correct date for religious observances and to assign Torah readings to particular days. A year generally runs from September to September. The year 5775 begins at sundown on September 24, 2014, and ends on sundown September 13, 2015.

Evidence of the Romans' influence on world culture still lingers. Some months of the year are named for Roman gods, including two emperors.

Month	Comes From	Who or What
January	Janus	God of Doors (for the first month of the year)
March	Mars	God of War (the month soldiers went to work; they did not fight in winter months)
May	Maia	Goddess of Growth
June	Juno	Queen of the Gods
July	Julius Caesar	He reorganized the calendar
August	Augustus Caesar	First emperor of the Roman Empire

JERUSALEM: HOLY CITY TO THE WORLD

THE CITY OF JERUSALEM IS IMPORTANT TO THREE MAJOR WORLD religions: Judaism, Christianity, and Islam.

Since biblical times, Jews have considered Jerusalem holy. The Western Wall, the only remains of the Second Temple, is one of the most sacred sites to Jews in Jerusalem. Each year, millions of locals and visitors come the wall to pray and often write prayers and tuck the papers into cracks in the wall. About twice a year, the written prayers are removed and buried in a cemetery on the Mount of Olives. It is forbidden to destroy anything that has the name of God written on it. People who cannot visit Jerusalem in person can send a prayer via e-mail through Aish.com's Wall Camera. Prayers will be printed out and placed in the wall by a yeshiva student.

Christians consider Jerusalem sacred because Jesus taught and died there. The Church of the Holy Sepulchre, built on the location of Jesus's crucifixion, is a sacred site in the city.

Jerusalem is one of three cities sacred to Muslims, after Mecca and Medina in Saudi Arabia. The Muslim holy prophet Muhammad is believed to have left from Jerusalem when he visited heaven. Today, the shrine known as the Dome of the Rock is on that site.

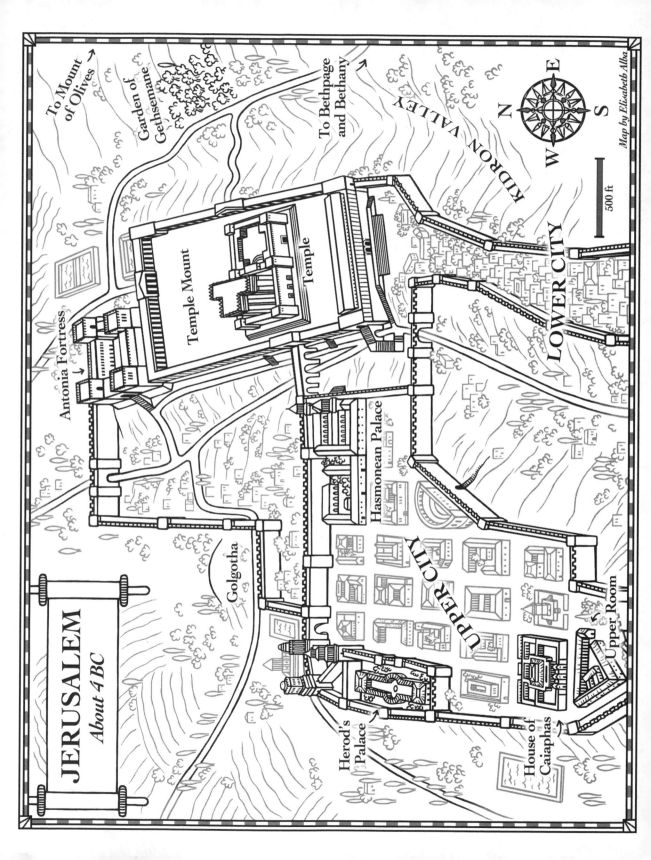

JERUSALEM
About 4 BC

To Mount of Olives →

Garden of Gethsemane

To Bethpage and Bethany →

KIDRON VALLEY

N
E
W
S

500 ft

Map by Elisabeth Alba

LOWER CITY

Temple Mount

Temple

Antonia Fortress

Hasmonean Palace

UPPER CITY

Golgotha

Herod's Palace

Upper Room

House of Caiaphas

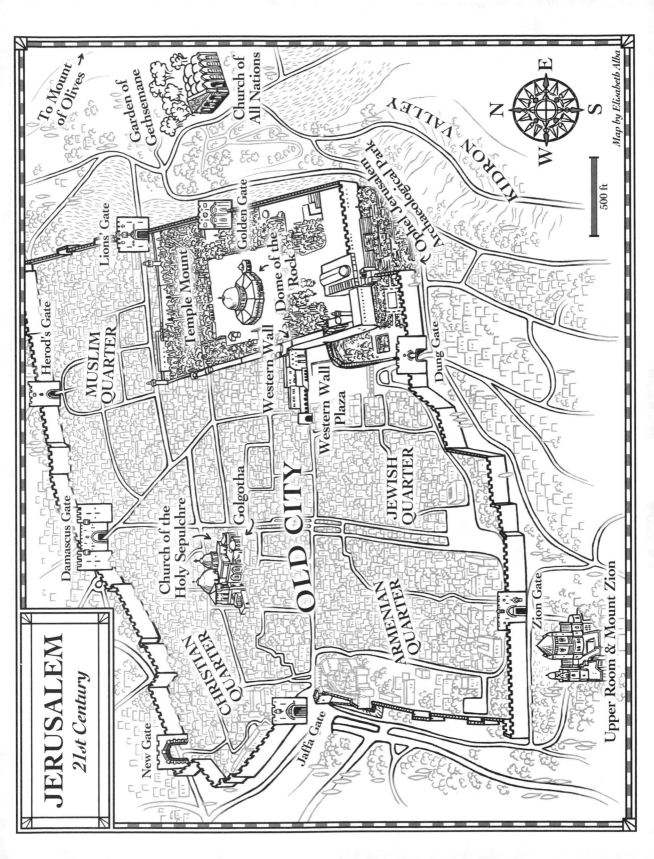

HOW WE KNOW ABOUT THE LIFE OF JESUS

The New Testament

The New Testament is the second half of the Christian Bible. It contains twenty-seven books written between AD 50 and AD 100 by followers of Jesus. Historians have identified the eight writers as six apostles—Matthew, John, Paul, James, Peter, and Jude—and two of their disciples, Mark and Luke.

The books of the New Testament can be divided into three groups: historical books that mostly relate the life of Jesus, though one, called Acts, details the establishment of early church communities in Palestine and Syria; morally instructive books that are letters to early Christian congregations;

A relief showing the symbols of the four gospel writers: John, an eagle; Luke, a winged bull; Matthew, an angel; and Mark, a winged lion.
[Mary Evans Picture Library]

and one prophetic book, the Apocalypse or Book of Revelation, which recounts a vision experienced by its writer, John.

The books were gathered together over time to form the document known as the New Testament. The accounts and quotes in this book are taken from the New International Version published by Zondervan in 2011.

Flavius Josephus

In addition to the New Testament, a contemporary historian named Flavius Josephus wrote a history of the Jewish people, called *Jewish Antiquities*. He was a well-educated Jew who grew up in Jerusalem. His history mentions Jesus several times and is used to provide historical evidence of some of the events in Jesus's life and what his followers believed him to be.

Flavius Josephus shown in a 19th-century engraving.
[The Bridgeman Art Library]

Tacitus

The Roman historian Gaius Cornelius Tacitus was also a senator. In about AD 116 he wrote an account of the empire that includes references to Jesus's condemnation by Pontius Pilate and his crucifixion.

Archaeological Evidence

There is a great deal of interest in life in the first century in what was the province of Judea. Sites in Jerusalem are excavated continually to show what architecture and living conditions might have been like. Historians examine fragments of pottery for food residue, bones for nutritional indicators, and walls for murals that may tell stories about beliefs and customs. It is a search that continues, with new findings every year. There are twenty-nine current digs in Israel, including ones in Tiberius and Mount Zion, in addition to those in Jordan, Italy, Spain, Turkey, and Egypt. To see a list of interesting digs, visit Biblicalarchaeology.org.

Gaius Cornelius Tacitus. Engraving; no date.
[The Bridgeman Art Library]

THE DEAD SEA SCROLLS

THE DISCOVERY OF A CAVE PROTECTING ANCIENT MANUSCRIPTS was the most exciting biblical find of the twentieth century. In 1947, Bedouin goatherds were searching for a lost goat in the hills along the Dead Sea. One threw a stone into a cave, and instead of a goat bolting, he heard the sound of a jar smashing. Alert for treasure, he entered the cave to find seven tall pottery jars. Inside were nearly intact scrolls and some fragments written on parchment and papyrus as well as one engraved copper tablet.

One of the Qumran caves where the Dead Sea Scrolls were found.
[Kurt Prescott]

By 1956, ten more caves had been found in the area now known as Khirbet Qumran. Scholars now have fragments of almost 900 documents dating from 250 BC to AD 68. Among them are the oldest known copies of the books of the Hebrew Bible written in Hebrew and Aramaic, as well as prayers, hymns, and other writings.

Although the Dead Sea Scrolls, as the mass of documents is known, do not mention Jesus, they are strong evidence of how important religion was in the lives of the people living in the area at Jesus's time. And they provide a wealth of information about first-century Judaism and the development of early Christianity.

You can browse the Dead Sea Scrolls and learn about the efforts to translate them at http://www.deadseascrolls.org.il/.

Limestone cliffs rise above the Dead Sea. [Library of Congress]

THE PURPLE CLOAK

THE ROBE WORN BY JESUS JUST BEFORE HIS CRUCIFIXION HAS captured the attention and the imagination of people for centuries. Its color was intended to mock him, signifying that he was "king of the Jews." What might that royal color have actually looked like?

In the first century, most cloth was the neutral color of the flax or wool from which it was woven. More vibrant hues were rare and valuable; there were three known to be extremely long-lasting and intense. In Hebrew, they are *tekhelet*, a bluish purple; *tola'at shani*, scarlet; and *argaman*, a reddish purple known to the Romans as Tyrian purple. While dye of the scarlet *tola'at shani* was made from an insect, dyes of the purplish *argaman* and *tekhelet* were made from mollusks, animals such as snails or oysters.

Archaeological researchers have discovered large numbers of mollusk shells throughout the Mediterranean. In particular, they found many shells in modern Lebanon near the cities of Tyre and Sidon, which were centers of the manufacture of dye in the time of Jesus. Dye makers collected the animals and punctured the shells, pulling the creatures out. Then the juices from their stomachs were drained. These contained the valuable pigment—the source of the color. Experiments have shown that liquid taken from twelve thousand mollusks produces only .053 ounce (1.5 grams) of pure purple dye. For this reason, a pound of Tyrian purple cost the equivalent of roughly ten thousand dollars. Because it was so valuable, it truly was the color of kings.

A lithograph showing varieties of mollusks. [The Bridgeman Art Library]

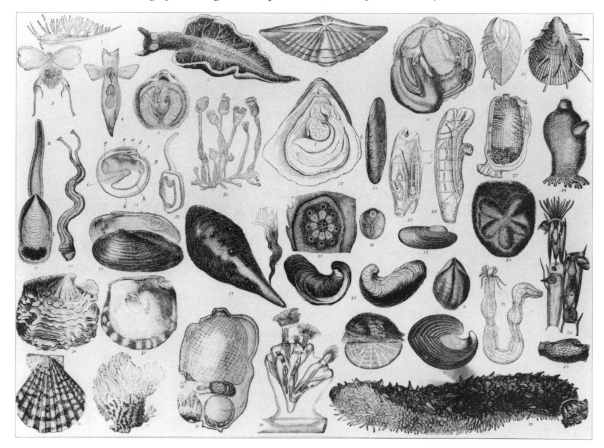

THE SYMBOL OF THE CROSS

FOR YEARS AFTER THE DEATH OF Jesus, Christians were embarrassed by the cross, for it was considered a cause of death best suited for slaves, murderers, and members of the lowest class. However, by the second century, Christians began touching their forehead, chest, and each shoulder to make the sign of the cross as a way of warding off demons. By the fourth century, the cross was more commonly viewed with pride, as a symbol that Jesus had suffered a lowly death for the benefit of all mankind. The iconic image showing the body of Jesus affixed to a cross did not become part of the Christian culture until six centuries after his death.

A 12th-century cross from a monastery in Spain. [The Bridgeman Art Library]

THIRTY PIECES OF SILVER: HOW MUCH IS THAT WORTH?

JUDAS ISCARIOT ACCEPTED THIRTY PIECES OF SILVER AS PAYment for betraying Jesus to the Romans. Was that a lot of money or a little? It is difficult to know exactly.

The kind of silver coin that Judas received was most likely referred to as a *shekel*. This kind of shekel is a coin that weighs about a half ounce of silver. A shekel was a unit of weight, so one could also have a shekel of grain or a shekel of spices.

In Jesus's day, thirty shekel coins might buy a slave who would work for you until he had saved up enough money to buy his freedom. For a skilled laborer, thirty shekels would be about four to six months' wages.

Thirty coins was very likely a huge amount for Judas, especially considering the scarcity of actual money at the time. Despite that, according to a gospel account in the New Testament, when Judas heard that Jesus had been killed, he returned to the temple and threw down the thirty coins. It is said that the priests used the coins to buy a field to be used as a cemetery for foreigners.

A WORLD OF MANY TONGUES: LANGUAGES IN FIRST-CENTURY JUDEA

THE SIGN THAT WAS NAILED TO THE CROSS ABOVE Jesus's head was written in Greek, Aramaic, and Latin.

In the Roman Empire, with its vast area and many conquered peoples, trade and travel among peoples was common. It was usual for a person to know more than one language. Jesus would have understood several languages and been able to read another.

In Galilee, the predominant spoken language in the first century was Aramaic, a language related to Hebrew and Arabic. Growing up in Nazareth, one of Jesus's tasks would have been to learn enough Hebrew to read aloud from the Scriptures. Most scholars agree that Hebrew was not a commonly spoken language at the time.

Roman soldiers spoke Latin, and it is likely that Jesus knew enough to understand some of what soldiers said. Pilate spoke Latin as his first language, and Herod must have spoken fluently too. Some historians think that Jesus's trial was conducted in Latin.

Greek was used in trade and business. Since Jesus and Joseph may have worked in Sepphoris, they may have needed to know some Greek. Also, Capernaum, the city Jesus used as the base for his ministry, was a big trading center where several languages would have been heard.

Ancient alphabets, from left, Hebrew, Phoenician, Ancient Greek, Later Greek, English, and Hebrew used on coins.
[North Wind Picture Library]

SOME FACTS ABOUT THE FIRST CENTURY AD

THE POPULATION OF THE WORLD IN THE YEAR AD I IS THOUGHT to have been between 170 and 400 million. That is a huge range, but of course historians don't have accurate population counts except for large cities in organized empires such as Rome's. (The world population in October 2013 was about 7.2 billion.)

Percent of World Population

	AD 1	2010
Asia	69%	60.3%
Europe	18%	10.7%
Africa	10%	14.9%
Latin America/ Caribbean	*	8.6%
North America	*	5.0%
Oceania	*	0.5%

*The combined population of Latin America, the Caribbean, North America, and Oceania was 3% of the total world population of about 200 million people. Today the world population exceeds 7 billion with 200,000 people born every day.

Major World Cities Between 100 BC and AD 100

Alexandria, Egypt

Chang'an (Xi'an), China

Constantinople (Istanbul), Turkey

Pataliputra, India

Rome, Italy

THE ROMAN EMPIRE IN 44 BC

T HE MAP ON THE NEXT PAGE SHOWS WHAT THE ROMAN EMPIRE
looked like during the life of Jesus. At the height of its powers in
AD 117, the Roman Empire covered 2.5 million square miles in
three continents: Europe, Asia, and Africa.

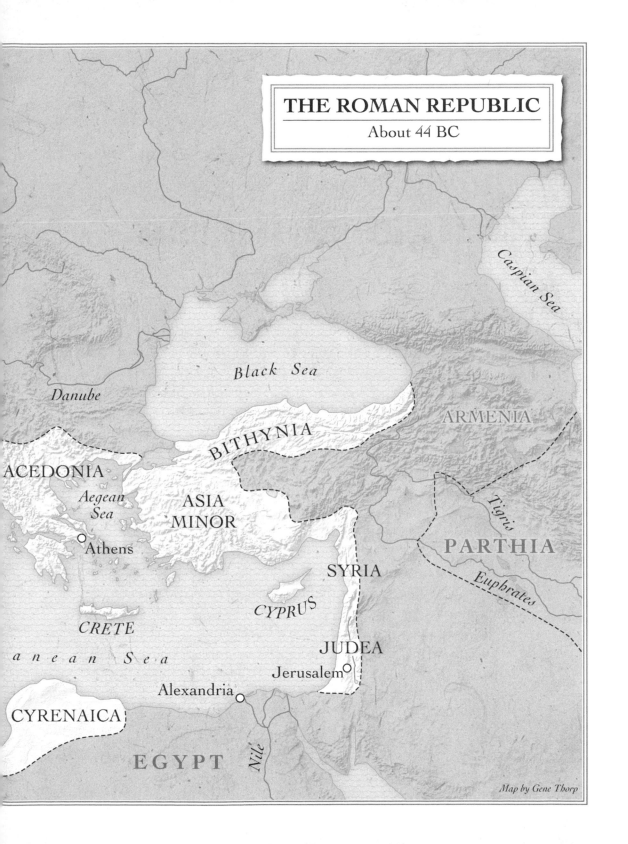

THE ROMAN REPUBLIC
About 44 BC

Caspian Sea

Black Sea

Danube

ARMENIA

BITHYNIA

ACEDONIA

Aegean Sea

ASIA MINOR

Tigris

PARTHIA

○ Athens

SYRIA

Euphrates

CYPRUS

CRETE

JUDEA

a n e a n   S e a

Jerusalem ○

Alexandria ○

CYRENAICA

Nile

EGYPT

Map by Gene Thorp

ROMAN GOVERNMENT AND CITIZENS

A S SOON AS OCTAVIAN BECAME EMPEROR IN 12 BC, HE was renamed Augustus. One of his first acts was to declare that his predecessor, Julius Caesar, was a god. Caesar's name was added to the numbers of gods the Romans worshipped, the top three being Jupiter, Juno, and Minerva. This began what is called the imperial cult, worshipping a person in government as a god. Augustus himself took the title *divi filius,* "son of the divine." Purple was the color of power in the Roman Empire, and the **emperor** was the only person allowed to wear a purple toga.

Below the emperor were **senators,** eight hundred men who met to decide matters of law. These men and their families were considered to be the noble men and women of the empire. But they served at the will of the emperor, so if they misstepped, they might be banished. Senators wore tunics with wide purple stripes.

The **equestrians** were originally members of the Roman cavalry. By 200 BC, the class had evolved to be primarily businessmen who could

Roman senators outside a temple. A 4th-century marble frieze. [The Bridgeman Art Library]

prove that they had a certain amount of money. If an equestrian took a political job, he could move up to the senatorial class. Equestrians wore tunics with narrow purple stripes.

Members of the **common class** were freeborn Roman citizens. They might be tradespeople like Joseph, farmers, fishermen, or small businessmen. They wore togas.

Junius Latins were former slaves who had been freed by Roman citizens. They had some rights but not the right of full citizenship unless they joined the legionnaires.

Foreigners were all the other free people who lived in the Roman Empire. Some foreigners were considered *socii*, or allies. In Jesus's time, socii had some basic rights and could be conscripted into the Roman army. If Jesus had been a full citizen of the Roman Empire he would have been killed by another method, not crucifixion. Roman citizens could not be crucified. In AD 212, the socii revolted and were given full citizenship.

Liberati were former slaves who had purchased their own freedom. Their former owners were now called their patrons and still had some control over them. This status lasted for one generation. A liberati's child would be truly free.

Slaves were either born into slavery, captured during wars, or sold into slavery by traders.

It was possible, by accumulating wealth, to move up from the common class to the equestrian class. And eventually, a very few equestrians were named to the senate.

ROMAN RELIGION

Athena, known in Roman mythology as Minerva. Roman copy of a 4th-century marble statue. [The Bridgeman Art Library]

THE TINY LAND OF THE JEWS WAS surrounded by nations that worshipped differently than they did. Unique to the many peoples of the Roman Empire, the Jews worshipped one God. The other active civilizations around them worshipped many gods.

The Roman pantheon, the group of officially recognized gods, was huge. There were the major gods, and then hundreds of minor gods. There were gods for places, such as rivers and towns; for work, such as pottery and farming; for attributes, such as courage and humor; and for relationships, such as marriage and children. The greatest three of all the gods were Jupiter, the king of the gods; his wife, Juno; and Minerva, the goddess of wisdom.

The Romans chose their gods from the Latins, who lived in what is now Italy, and from the Greeks. For example, in Greek mythology, Zeus and Hera were the king and queen of the gods. They had different names but almost the same backgrounds and histories as Jupiter and Juno.

Over time, tales about the Roman gods, their wars and relationships, developed into long and complicated soap operas. Parents passed down stories to their children, sculptors carved scenes from the tales, and poets and musicians wrote of the goings-on in the kingdom of the gods.

Every Roman home had a small shrine devoted to a household god. Bits of food were left for the god or goddess or the household spirit. There were seasonal celebrations to honor gods and goddesses, and temples and shrines were built on every road and in every town.

When Augustus Caesar became emperor in 27 BC, he declared that he was the son of a god. And so the emperors joined the pantheon of gods and increased their power over all their subjects.

ROMAN LEGIONNAIRES: THE ARMY THAT CONQUERED GALILEE AND JUDEA

D URING THE YEARS OF THE ROMAN EMPIRE, beginning in 31 BC, the Roman army was a vast force controlling most of the Mediterranean area. There were commanders, of course, who reported to the emperor. But the ones on the ground were the famous legionnaires, who fought in units of 3,000 to 6,000 men. Men of Roman birth and freed slaves could become legionnaires. (As soon as a freed slave was admitted to the legionnaires, he automatically became a citizen.)

Legionnaires carried javelins and short swords. They formed up for battle in phalanxes, rows of men eight to ten deep, walking close together. When they got near their enemy, they threw their javelins and rushed in. The battles were fierce and resulted in huge numbers of casualties. Legionnaires worshipped Mars, the god of war.

Statue of a legionnaire at the Museum of Roman Civilization in Rome, Italy. [The Bridgeman Art Library]

ROMAN ROADS

THE ROMANS WERE FAMOUS FOR THE ROADS THEY BUILT. SOME are still used today, two thousand years later! And it was the legionnaires, along with prisoners of war and slaves, who did the hard work of building thousands of miles of roads that connected the faraway provinces of the Roman Empire. Roads helped messages and news travel, brought goods and food to cities from farmland and harbors, and allowed armies to travel quickly from place to place when needed. Built to a uniform width of 5 meters (5.46 yards), the Roman roads were wide enough for two wagons to pass each other.

Each road began with a layer of sand, followed by stone slabs, crushed stone in cement, and finally stone blocks, often called paving blocks. Drainage ditches were built on both sides of the road. Once the road was built, the locality through which it passed was charged with maintaining it. Soon rest areas, inns, and places to eat sprang up along the roads, providing local people with income from travelers.

A surviving Roman paved road near Tuscany in Italy. [The Bridgeman Art Library]

A WALK THROUGH TWENTY-FIRST-CENTURY JERUSALEM

RECENT EXCAVATIONS HAVE UNCOVERED SOME OF THE ACTUAL streets and homes of Jesus's time, allowing visitors to walk in his footsteps and glimpse what life was like in Jerusalem in the first century AD.

King David founded Jerusalem more than three thousand years ago as his royal city. It is where the temples of the Jewish kings Solomon and Herod once stood. Today it is called the Eternal City and holds a special place in Jewish, Islamic, and Christian religions. The history of the city is rich, though filled with conflicts. The sights, archaeological evidence, and modern history are fascinating. Below are places you can visit that are mentioned in this book.

Let's start outside the city on the **MOUNT OF OLIVES.** This is where Jesus often paused to teach his disciples. It offers a spectacular view of the Old City of Jerusalem, the Temple Mount area, and the new city.

On the Mount of Olives, the **CHURCH OF THE PATER NOSTER** is built on the site where Jesus is said to have taught his disciples the "Our Father" prayer. There is a plaque there with the prayer translated into more than a hundred languages.

At the foot of the Mount of Olives is the **GARDEN OF GETHSEMANE,** where Jesus spent time in solitary prayer and was betrayed by Judas and arrested by the Romans. Today it is the site of the Church of All Nations. The olive trees in the garden are thought to be nine hundred years old.

Walking across the Kidron Valley, you approach the seven gates that lead into the **OLD CITY.** Today, the Old City is home to 35,000 people—about 26,000 Muslims, 6,000 Christians, and 3,000 Jews. The population of the whole city of Jerusalem is about 800,000. In 2011, there were 497,000 Jews, 281,000 Muslims, 14,000 Christians, and 9,000 who stated no religion.

You can see remains of the steps leading up to the temple in the Ophel Archaeological Park. The only remnant of Herod's temple is the huge **WESTERN WALL.**

The Golden Dome Mosque on Temple Mount. [Shutterstock]

The **CENACLE,** on Mount Zion, is the traditional site of the Upper Room where Jesus held his last supper for his disciples. Today this building houses a tomb, a yeshiva, a church, a mosque, and a kindergarten. Mount Zion was the Upper City of Jerusalem in Jesus's day and was inside the city walls.

The path that Jesus walked began at **HEROD'S PALACE,** near what is now the Jaffa Gate. It ends at the **CHURCH OF THE HOLY SEPULCHRE,** which is thought to have been built atop the site of Golgotha and near Jesus's tomb. Today, visitors can tour these sites and even touch the place where the cross of Jesus is said to have once rested.

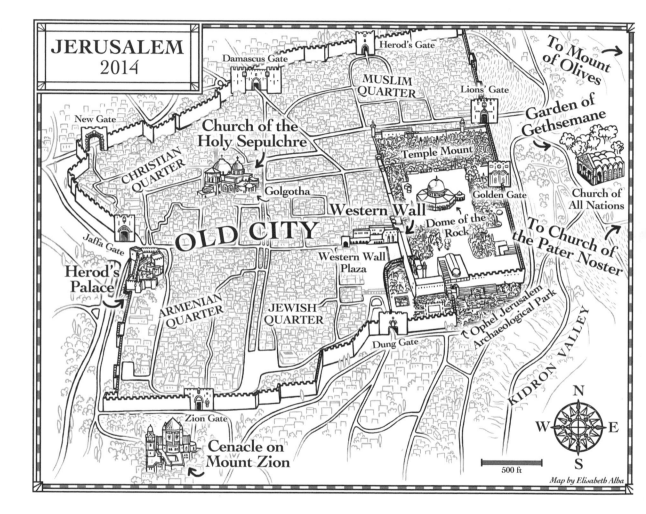

JERUSALEM
2014

New Gate

Damascus Gate

Herod's Gate

MUSLIM
QUARTER

Lions' Gate

To Mount
of Olives

CHRISTIAN
QUARTER

Church of the
Holy Sepulchre

Temple Mount

Garden of
Gethsemane

Golgotha

Golden Gate

Church of
All Nations

OLD CITY

Western Wall

Dome of the
Rock

To Church of
the Pater Noster

Jaffa Gate

Western Wall
Plaza

Herod's
Palace

ARMENIAN
QUARTER

JEWISH
QUARTER

Ophel Jerusalem
Archaeological Park

Dung Gate

KIDRON VALLEY

Zion Gate

N

W   E

S

Cenacle on
Mount Zion

500 ft

Map by Elisabeth Alba

GLOSSARY

Aloe: A fragrant resin from the *Aquilaria agallocha* tree.

Apostle: One who travels to represent beliefs or teachings.

Asia Minor: The peninsula between the Black Sea, the Mediterranean Sea, and the Aegean Sea.

Barracks: The building or buildings where soldiers live.

Bazaar: A street market.

Benefactor: One who makes a gift.

Blasphemy: The act of saying offensive things about God or a religion.

Caravan: A group of people or vehicles traveling together.

Card: To clean and untangle wool before spinning it into thread.

Charisma: A powerful personal appeal that attracts people.

Circumcise: To cut off the foreskin.

Citadel: A fortress that commands a city.

Cloister: A covered walkway with columns.

Crucify: To put to death by nailing hands, wrists, feet, or ankles to a cross.

Devout: Deeply religious.

Disciple: A student or pupil who helps to spread a teacher's doctrines.

Gentile: One who is not of the Jewish faith.

Graven image: An object of worship carved from wood or stone; an idol.

Heresy: Views different from those of a particular religion.

Hosanna: A Hebrew term used to express praise to God, used today by Jews and Christians.

Imperial: Having to do with the empire or emperor.

Leaven: A substance, such as yeast, that makes dough or batter rise.

Legionnaire: A Roman soldier; a member of a legion of 3,000 to 6,000 foot soldiers.

Levy: To impose or collect by lawful actions or by force.

Limestone: A rock used in building and to make cement, formed from the remains of shells and coral.

Magi: The legendary wise men who visited Jesus soon after he was born.

Messiah: The expected king and deliverer of the Jews.

Mikvah: A ritual purification bath taken on certain occasions, such as before celebrating Passover.

Myrrh: A fragrant gum resin from various trees in the genus *Commiphora*.

Parable: A fable or story that conveys a moral or religious lesson.

Parchment: Heavy, paperlike writing material made from the skin of sheep or goats.

Passover: An important Jewish holiday that celebrates the Jews' escape from slavery in Egypt.

Patriarch: The male head of a family or tribe, or an older man in a village, group, or tribe who is respected and holds a place of honor.

Persecute: To continually treat someone cruelly and unfairly, especially because of that person's ideas or political beliefs.

Pilgrim: Someone who journeys to a holy place to worship.

Prophet: One who speaks or claims to speak for God; someone who predicts what will happen in the future.

Psalm: A sacred song written down in the Book of Psalms in the Jewish Tanakh and Christian Bible.

Rabbi: A Jewish religious leader and teacher.

Repent: To turn away from sin and agree to change one's life.

Resin: A yellow or brown sticky substance that oozes from some trees, used to make polishes, glue, and incense, among other things.

Sabbath: A day of rest and worship that, for the Jews, takes place from sundown on Friday to sundown on Saturday.

Sage: A wise person.

Scourge: To punish severely, especially by whipping.

Scribe: A person who copies books by hand.

Scripture: A sacred body of writing; usually applied to the Bible.

Seder: A Jewish service including a dinner held on Passover.

Serenity: The state of being calm and peaceful.

Shekel: An ancient Hebrew coin that was the only legal currency in the temple; also a unit of weight.

Slaver: Someone who steals, captures, or kidnaps people to sell them into slavery.

Synagogue: A building used by Jewish people for worship and religious study.

Tanakh: The Hebrew Bible, which contains the Torah, Nevi'im (or Prophets), and Ketuvim (other writings).

Tassel: A bunch of cords or threads tied together at the top and then sewn onto clothing or used as decoration.

Temple Mount: A 36-acre structure in the Old City of Jerusalem, including surrounding walls, courtyards, and the temple, that has been used and revered by Jews, Muslims, and Christians.

Terrace: A series of steps or ridges built into a hillside so crops can be planted on them.

Torah: The sacred scroll on which is written in Hebrew the books of Genesis, Exodus, Leviticus, Numbers, and Deuteronomy.

Tyrant: Someone who rules in a cruel or unjust way.

TIME LINE OF JESUS'S LIFE

We cannot be sure of the exact dates below. Scientists and archaeologists continue to try to pinpoint the year of Jesus's birth and, therefore, death.

6 BC John the Baptist is born (he is about six months older than Jesus).

6–5 BC Jesus is born in Bethlehem in Judea.

5 BC Herod the Great orders the massacre of all male children in Bethlehem under two years of age.

AD 6 Herod Antipas is appointed tetrarch of Galilee.

AD 7 Jesus, age twelve, visits the temple in Jerusalem.

AD 14 Tiberius becomes emperor and will rule until his death in AD 37.

AD 25 Caiaphas succeeds his father-in-law, Annas, as high priest at the temple in Jerusalem.

AD 26 Pontius Pilate is named prefect, or governor, of Judea.

AD 26 John the Baptist establishes his ministry.

AD 27 Jesus turns the moneylenders away from the temple.

AD 27   Jesus delivers the Sermon on the Mount.

AD 29   John the Baptist is beheaded.

Sunday, April 1,   Jesus makes a triumphal entry into Jerusalem.
AD 30

Thursday,   Jesus shares supper with his disciples.
April 5, AD 30

Friday, April 6,   Jesus is put to death by crucifixion.
AD 30

An illustration of Nazareth from a German book
published in 1902. [Mary Evans Picture Library]

THE AUTHOR RECOMMENDS . . .

Recommended Reading

Ackroyd, Peter. *Ancient Rome: Voyages Through Time*. New York: DK, 2005.

Anderson, Michael, ed. *Ancient Rome*. New York: Britannica Educational Publishing, 2012.

Blacklock, Dyan. *The Roman Army: The Legendary Soldiers Who Created an Empire*. New York: Walker & Co., 2004.

Cefrey, Holly. *Archaeologists: Life Digging Up Artifacts*. New York: Rosen Central, 2004.

Deckker, Zilah. *National Geographic Investigates Ancient Rome: Archaeology Unlocks the Secrets of Rome's Past*. Washington, DC: National Geographic, 2007.

Gedacht, Daniel. *Technology of Ancient Rome*. New York: PowerKids Press, 2004.

Harik, Ramsay M. *Jesus of Nazareth: Teacher and Prophet*. New York: Franklin Watts, 2001.

Hoffman, Ya'ir. *The World of the Bible for Young Readers*. New York: Viking, 1989.

Korb, Scott. *Life in Year One: What the World Was Like in First-Century Palestine*. New York: Riverhead Books, 2010.

Mason, Anthony. *Biblical Times*. New York: Simon & Schuster Books for Young Readers, 1996.

Nardo, Don. *Life of a Roman Slave*. San Diego: Lucent Books, 1998.

———. *Life of a Roman Soldier.* San Diego: Lucent Books, 2001.

———. *Roman Roads and Aqueducts.* San Diego: Lucent Books, 2001.

———. *Life During Great Civilizations: Ancient Rome.* Farmington Hills, MI: Blackbirch Press, 2003.

Sherman, Josepha. *Your Travel Guide to Ancient Israel.* Minneapolis: Lerner Publications, 2004.

Winter, Jonah. *Peaceful Heroes.* New York: Scholastic, Inc., 2009.

Recommended Websites

Frontline, "From Jesus to Christ: The First Christians": pbs.org/wgbh/pages/frontline/shows/religion.

The Jesus Seminar Forum: virtualreligion.net/forum.

Into His Own: Perspective on the World of Jesus: virtualreligion.net/iho.

Recommended Viewing

In Search of Easter. National Geographic Video, 2004.

In the Footsteps of the Holy Family. A&E Home Video, 2001.

ABC News Presents Peter Jennings Reporting: The Search for Jesus. ABC TV, 2000.

The Story of Jesus. BBC, 2011.

Who Was Jesus? Discovery Channel, 2010.

BIBLIOGRAPHY

The Holy Bible: New International Version. Grand Rapids, Mich.: Zondervan Publishing House, 2011.

Aslan, Reza. *Zealot: The Life and Times of Jesus of Nazareth*. New York: Random House, 2013.

Borg, Marcus J., and John Dominic Crossan. *The Last Week: A Day-by-Day Account of Jesus's Final Week in Jerusalem*. New York: Harper San Francisco, 2006.

Brenner, Michael. *A Short History of the Jews*. Princeton: Princeton University Press, 2010.

Cahill, Thomas. *Desire of the Everlasting Hills: The World Before and After Jesus*. New York: Random House, 1999.

Cantor, Norman F. *The Sacred Chain: The History of the Jews*. New York: HarperCollins, 1994.

Goodman, Martin. *Rome and Jerusalem: The Clash of Ancient Civilizations*. New York: Alfred A. Knopf, 2007.

Harik, Ramsay M. *Jesus of Nazareth: Teacher and Prophet*. New York: Franklin Watts, 2001.

Hoffman, Ya'ir. *The World of the Bible for Young Readers*. New York: Viking, 1989.

Johnson, Paul. *The History of the Jews*. New York: Harper & Row, 1987.

Korb, Scott. *Life in Year One: What the World Was Like in First-Century Palestine*. New York: Riverhead Books, 2010.

Lucie-Smith, Edward. *The Face of Jesus*. New York: Abrams, 2011.

O'Reilly, Bill, and Martin Dugard. *Killing Jesus: A History*. New York: Henry Holt, 2013.

Shorto, Russell. *Gospel Truth: The New Image of Jesus Emerging from Science and History and Why It Matters*. New York: Riverhead Books, 1997.

Wilson, Samantha. *Israel: The Brandt Travel Guide*. Guilford, CT: The Globe Pequot Press, 2009.

INDEX

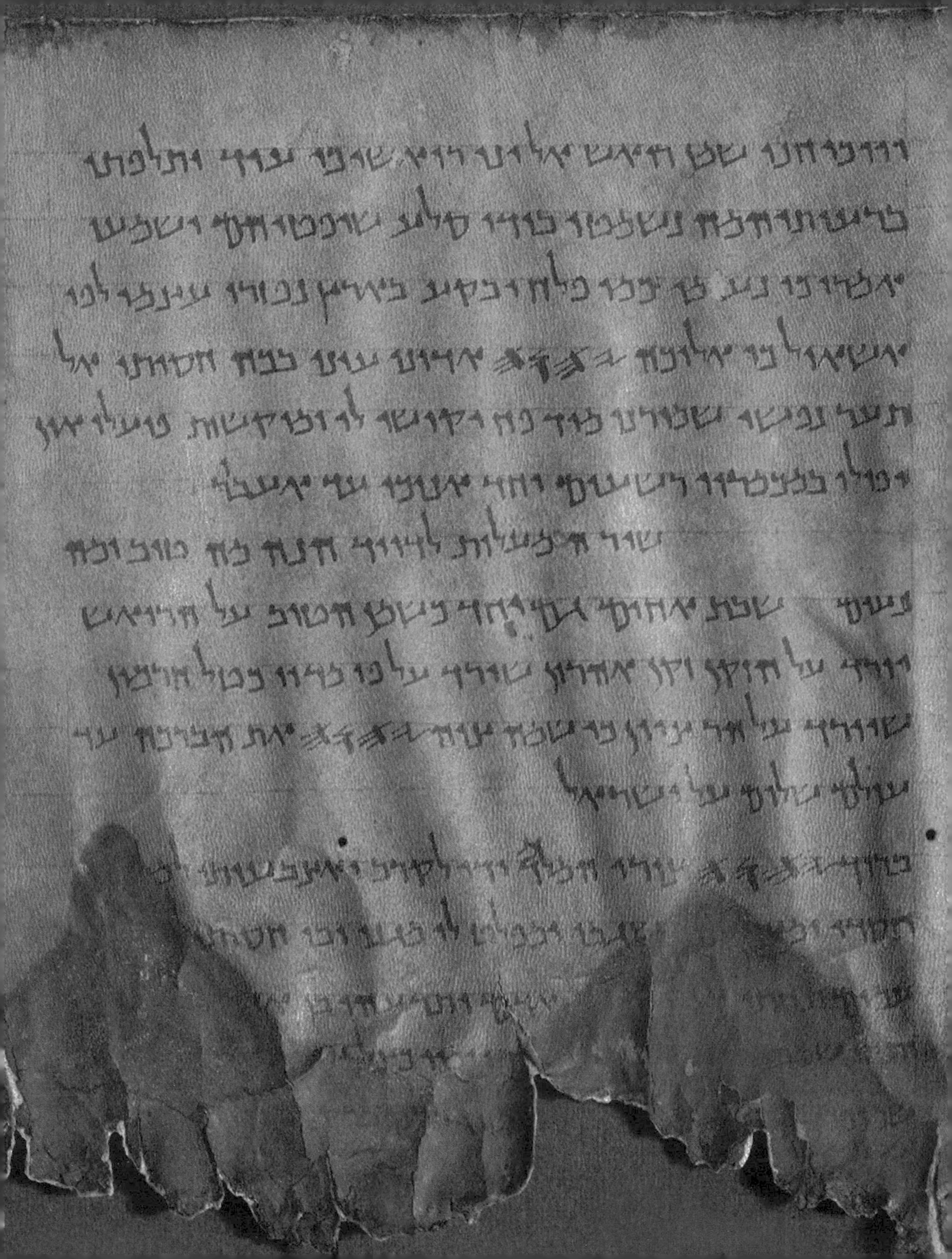